THE FOUNDLING MUSEUM

AN INTRODUCTION

The Foundling Museum
40 Brunswick Square
London, WC1N 1AZ
www.foundlingmuseum.org.uk

The Foundling Museum would like to thank John Styles for his contribution, Janette Bright and Gillian Clark for their research into the foundling stories, and the former pupils of the Foundling Hospital School for allowing us to include their testimonies and mementos of childhood. Thanks also go to Ralph Appelbaum Associates, staff at the London Metropolitan Archives and Coram for their assistance.

ISBN 978 0 9551808 9 7

British Library Cataloguing in Publication Data. A catalogue record for this book is available from the British Library.

Written by Caro Howell
Additional essay by John Styles
Designed by Joe Ewart, Society
Printed by Lamport Gilbert Ltd, Reading, Berkshire
Published by The Foundling Museum, London
Copyright © The Foundling Museum, 2014

Texts © 2014 the authors

Front cover: William Hogarth, Detail from *The March of the Guards to Finchley*, 1750. Secured for the Foundling Museum by the National Heritage Memorial Fund with a supporting contribution from the Art Fund in 2005 © The Foundling Museum

Inside front and back cover: *Foundling Back to Front Weekend by Yinka Shonibare MBE* © The Foundling Museum

All images © Coram in the care of the Foundling Museum except:
figs 1, 2, 11, 12, 15, 20, 25, 43, 57, 62 © The Foundling Museum
figs 5, 6, 7, 17, 21, 26, 30, 37, 45, 51, 58, 60 © Coram
figs 9, 46, 47, 48, 50, 53 © Gerald Coke Handel Foundation
fig 3 © Trustees of the British Museum
fig 16 Courtesy of Frank Butterworth
fig 52 © David Shrigley
fig 54 Image courtesy Tracey Emin Studio
fig 55 © Jacqueline Wilson
fig 56 © Clare Twomey
fig 59 By permission of the Folger Shakespeare Library
fig 63 Courtesy of Brian Girling

Supported by The Friends of Thomas Coram

Supported using public funding by
LOTTERY FUNDED | ARTS COUNCIL ENGLAND

CONTENTS

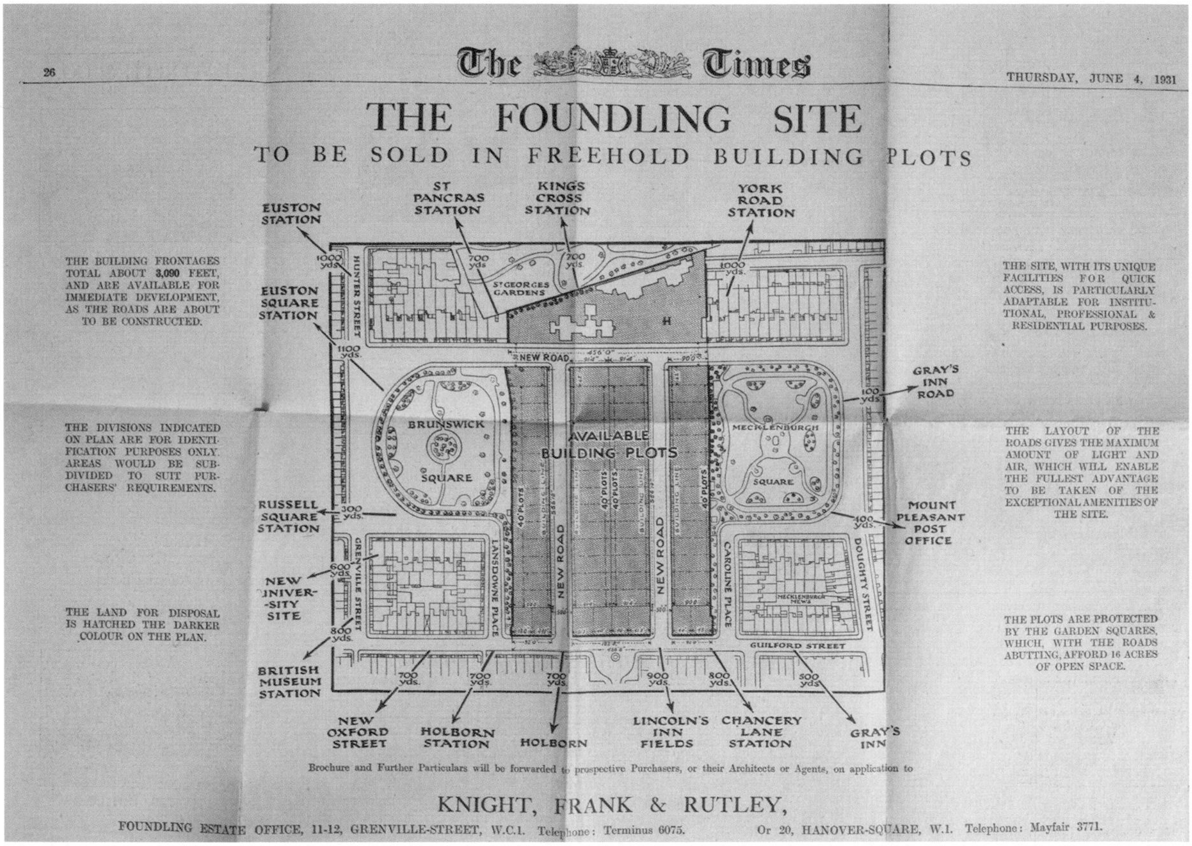

26 **The Times** THURSDAY, JUNE 4, 1931

THE FOUNDLING SITE

TO BE SOLD IN FREEHOLD BUILDING PLOTS

THE BUILDING FRONTAGES TOTAL ABOUT **3,090** FEET, AND ARE AVAILABLE FOR IMMEDIATE DEVELOPMENT, AS THE ROADS ARE ABOUT TO BE CONSTRUCTED.

THE DIVISIONS INDICATED ON PLAN ARE FOR IDENTIFICATION PURPOSES ONLY. AREAS WOULD BE SUBDIVIDED TO SUIT PURCHASERS' REQUIREMENTS.

THE LAND FOR DISPOSAL IS HATCHED THE DARKER COLOUR ON THE PLAN.

THE SITE, WITH ITS UNIQUE FACILITIES FOR QUICK ACCESS, IS PARTICULARLY ADAPTABLE FOR INSTITUTIONAL, PROFESSIONAL & RESIDENTIAL PURPOSES.

THE LAYOUT OF THE ROADS GIVES THE MAXIMUM AMOUNT OF LIGHT AND AIR, WHICH WILL ENABLE THE FULLEST ADVANTAGE TO BE TAKEN OF THE EXCEPTIONAL AMENITIES OF THE SITE.

THE PLOTS ARE PROTECTED BY THE GARDEN SQUARES, WHICH, WITH THE ROADS ABUTTING, AFFORD 16 ACRES OF OPEN SPACE.

Brochure and Further Particulars will be forwarded to prospective Purchasers, or their Architects or Agents, on application to

KNIGHT, FRANK & RUTLEY,

FOUNDLING ESTATE OFFICE, 11-12, GRENVILLE-STREET, W.C.1. Telephone: Terminus 6075. Or 20, HANOVER-SQUARE, W.1. Telephone: Mayfair 3771.

Fig. 1
Sections for sale from the Foundling Hospital Estate, *The Times*, 1931

INTRODUCTION

The Foundling Museum is home to many amazing stories stretching back nearly 300 years; stories of heartbreak, hope, generosity, loss, resilience and imagination. Above all, the stories we tell are personal. While the Foundling celebrates remarkable individuals like Thomas Coram, William Hogarth and George Frideric Handel, we also bear witness to those whose names or voices are lost to us; particularly those of the mothers and their foundling children.

The stories we tell are not just historic, they are contemporary and urgent. It is humbling to be able to listen to the testimony of former pupils of the Foundling Hospital, which continues today as the children's charity Coram. Their experiences of the institution from the 1920s to the 1950s, largely unchanged from those of their eighteenth-century forebears, make history come alive. So too do the voices of the looked after and care-experienced young people we work with today. They remind us that childhood need cannot be consigned to history and sealed away in display cases. However, while acknowledging that the issues the Hospital sought to alleviate are ongoing, we also celebrate the fact that artists of all disciplines continue to get involved in improving young people's lives. The spirit of Hogarth and Handel lives on in the work of the many artists who support our programmes. They remind us that the arts do not just provide the visuals, the commentary and the soundtrack to our lives; they can change, challenge and improve them.

As the Museum celebrates its tenth birthday, we would like to take this opportunity to thank the many organisations and individuals, including visitors, who have helped us over the years. There is not an area of our work that has not benefited from the advice and encouragement of others. I would most particularly like to thank my predecessors, Rhian Harris and Lars Tharp; our President, Patrick Walker; Vice Presidents Brian Allen, Alan Borg and David Coke; current and former Trustees, especially Carolyn Steen and Jamie Korner; as well as staff and volunteers, past and present, for their unstinting support.

Caro Howell, Director

THE FOUNDLING HOSPITAL SITE

17 October 1739	Thomas Coram is given a Royal Charter, signed by King George II for the establishment of a 'Hospital for the Maintenance and Education of Exposed and Deserted Young Children'. 'Hospital' meant charitable institution, not medical facility.
December 1740	A lease is taken on a house in Hatton Garden. On 25 March 1741, the coat of arms designed by Hogarth is hung above the Hospital doors. That evening, the first 30 children are admitted.
October 1740	The Committee recommends the purchase of two fields belonging to the Earl of Salisbury near Lamb's Conduit Street, as the site for a purpose-built Hospital. After some negotiation, the Earl agrees to sell 56 acres for £6,500.
16 September 1742	Vice-President, John Milner lays the foundation stone.
October 1745	Children move into the completed West Wing of the Foundling Hospital. Building starts on the Chapel in 1748 and on the East Wing in 1749. By the time the Wing is completed in 1752, the Hospital is caring for 600 children. The Chapel opens in 1753.
25 November 1926	The Hospital Estate is sold for £1.65 million to a property speculator, James White, who intends to relocate Covent Garden Market to the site. Opposition from residents forces the site to be advertised for sale. The Hospital Governors repurchase the northern portion of the site to build a London headquarters.
21, 22 and 24 June 1926	Pupils leave the Foundling Hospital for summer camp. On 14 September they move to their temporary home, the former St Anne's School in Redhill.
9 July 1935	Some 300 children are transferred from Redhill to their new school in Berkhamsted, Hertfordshire.
1936	Coram's Fields opens; three quarters of the original Hospital site, including the entrance gates and colonnades, having been preserved as a playground for children.
1939	40 Brunswick Square opens as the Foundling Hospital's London headquarters, containing the reassembled Court Room, Picture Gallery, Committee Room, staircase and many other fixtures from the original 1740s building.
1954	The last Foundling Hospital pupils removed from the school and placed in foster care.
June 2004	The Foundling Museum opens.

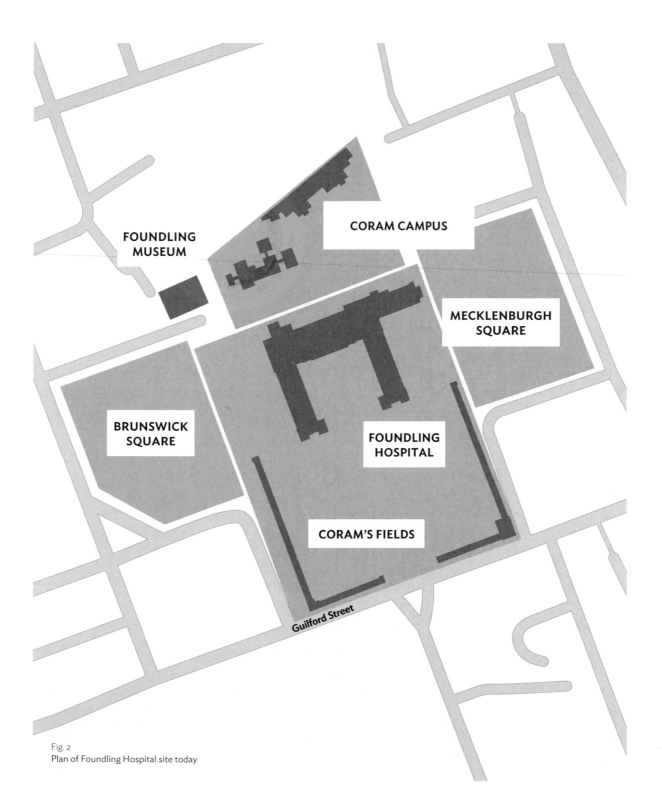

FOUNDLING
MUSEUM

CORAM CAMPUS

MECKLENBURGH
SQUARE

BRUNSWICK
SQUARE

FOUNDLING
HOSPITAL

CORAM'S FIELDS

Guilford Street

Fig. 2
Plan of Foundling Hospital site today

GIN LANE.

Gin cursed Fiend, with Fury fraught,
Makes human Race a Prey.
It enters by a deadly Draught,
And steals our Life away.

Virtue and Truth, driv'n to Despair,
Its Rage compells to fly,
But cherishes with hellish Care,
Theft, Murder, Perjury.

Damn'd Cup! that on the Vitals preys,
That liquid Fire contains,
Which Madness to the Heart conveys,
And rolls it thro' the Veins.

Price 1ˢ

THE FOUNDLING HOSPITAL STORY

When Thomas Coram (1668-1751) returned to London in 1704 after eleven years in America, it was to a city that was a powerhouse of industry, invention, global trade and wealth. It was also noisy, disease-ridden, polluted and the site of desperate poverty. The city's population was increasing rapidly, growing from an estimated 600,000 in 1700 to around a million by the end of the century. London's relentless expansion was fuelled by rural migration. However, removed from the moral and social support of their communities, many people fell into destitution and crime. Those who couldn't work were reliant on the Poor Law system of parish relief or, from 1722, the workhouse. With parishes unable to cope with demand and parishioners reluctant to contribute more, conditions for receiving help became increasingly stringent; so much so that churchwardens were allowed to hire out pauper children as apprentices, regardless of their suitability. Attitudes to poverty became increasingly harsh; crime was linked to idleness, destitution seen as a sign of moral weakness and distinctions were made between the deserving and the undeserving poor.

The situation for children was particularly bleak. In the early 1700s the mortality rate for the under fives was around 75%; in workhouses it was over 90%. The city was in the grip of the Gin Craze, and by 1730 London was distilling around ten million gallons annually. Since gin was both cheap and an appetite suppressant, poor mothers gave it to babies to keep them docile, leading to thousands of children dying of alcohol poisoning each year. Parents who were unable to care for their babies due to poverty or illegitimacy had few options, and many chose to abandon them in the street, outside churches and even on rubbish heaps. It is estimated that around a thousand babies a year were abandoned in London. Despite this, Londoners were loath to provide for foundlings. Illegitimacy carried the stigma of immorality and many believed that debauchery would be encouraged if 'the wages of sin' were supported, while parishes would escape their responsibilities. In Coram's 1737 petition to the King he paints a vivid picture of the situation:

... the frequent Murders committed on poor Miserable Infant Children at their Birth by their Cruel Parents to hide their Shame and for the Inhumane Custom of exposing New born children to Perish in the Streets or the putting out such unhappy Foundlings to wicked and barbarous Nurses who under-taking to bring them up for a Small and trifling Sum of Money do often suffer them to Starve for want of due Sustenance and Care Or if permitted to live either turn them into the Streets to begg or steal or Hire them out to Vicious Persons by whom they are trained up in that infamous way of living Whereby Thefts Robberys and Murders do grievously abound, and some of those Miserable Infants are Blinded or Maimed or Distorted in their Limbs in order to move Pity and

Opposite:
Fig. 3
William Hogarth, *Gin Lane*, 1751

Compassion and thereby become the fitter Instruments of gain to those Vile, Mercyless Wretches.

The situation was very different abroad. Across Europe organisations existed to care for abandoned and orphaned children, run by the Catholic Church. The *Hôpital des Enfants-Trouvés* in Paris was founded in 1670; the *Ospedale degli Innocenti* in Florence in 1419 and Rome's *Conservatorio della Ruota* dated back to the thirteenth century. Ironically, it was Britain's continuous warring with its continental neighbours that would provide a pragmatic argument for the foundling cause; the country needed fighting men and the military were not squeamish about their origins.

Despite the clear need for practical action, it took the dogged determination of one man to overcome moral qualms and social apathy, to ensure a better future for some of London's most vulnerable inhabitants. This man was Thomas Coram.

Thomas Coram and the Foundling Hospital Campaign

Coram was born in Lyme Regis, Dorset in about 1668, to a family that was humble but respectable. His father is believed to have been a master mariner and his mother died when he was six. At eleven, Coram was sent to sea for five years, before being apprenticed to a shipwright in London.

Despite this harsh start in life, he equipped himself well as a seaman and trader. So much so that aged 25, he left for Boston, USA with a cargo of goods and a team of shipwrights, to set up business and secure oak for the Navy. Initially, things went well. He established the first ship building business in Taunton, south of Boston and in 1700 made a good marriage to a Bostonian, Eunice Wayte. However, Coram's plain speaking and Anglicanism did not go down well with everyone. He was involved in a series of disputes that led to court cases, the burning of his ships and even an attempt on his life.

Fig. 4
Balthasar Nebot (fl. 1737-1762), *Captain Coram*. This painting was stolen from the Collection in the early 1990s, prior to the opening of the Museum

On returning to London in 1704, Coram continued in the shipbuilding business and to trade with the colonies. He was involved in breaking the Swedish Tar monopoly and in growing hemp along the New England coast. Comfortably well off, he moved to Rotherhithe, East London, in around 1720. However, on his journeys into London he was appalled by the sight of starving and abandoned children. Although childless himself, Coram decided to do something to rectify the situation and his relentless campaigning would occupy the next seventeen years of his life.

Coram had already shown himself to be unafraid of championing unpopular causes. In America he had tried, unsuccessfully, to set up a colony for destitute ex-soldiers; to convert Nonconformists to Anglicanism; to give Mohicans land rights; and to challenge the laws of primogeniture. In a New England court, an adversary of Coram's would prophetically testify that he was 'a man of that obstinate, persevering temper, as never to desist from his first enterprise, whatever obstacles lie in his way.' This was fortunate because without the benefits of rank, education and wealth, when it came to influencing society's opinion-formers, Coram had his work cut out.

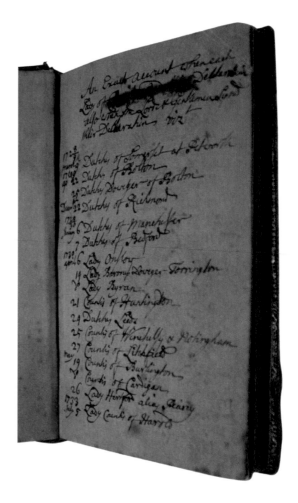

To set up a Foundling Hospital, Coram needed a Charter of Incorporation from the King. To achieve this, he required the support of the great and the good. However, there was no template for how to go about such a mission. His solution was to make a list of every influential individual and systematically lobby them one by one and in person. Coram's pocket book graphically illustrates the number of people he approached; he claimed he could walk ten or twelve miles a day across London collecting signatures. It is testament to his ingenuity and good sense that many of his strategies are standard practice for charities today – networking, peer-pressure and a powerful board.

Fig. 5
A page from Thomas Coram's pocket book showing a list of supporters, c.1720-39

Initial attempts to engage high-ranking members of the Church and the nobility met with little success. Coram then had the novel idea of approaching respectable ladies and appealing to their emotions. The growing fashion for sentiment and benevolence provided fertile ground for Coram's lobbying. In 1729 the Duchess of Somerset signed Coram's petition, paving the way for other ladies of fashion to follow suit. Thus the first petition to the King in 1735 came from 21 'Ladies of Quality and Distinction'. With wives and daughters putting pressure on the men in their lives, a second petition followed in 1737 from 'Noblemen and Gentlemen'. This included 25 dukes, 31 earls, 26 members of the peerage and 38 knights, along with the entire Privy Council which included the Prince of Wales, The Prime Minister, The Speaker of the House of Commons and the Justices of the Peace; 375 signatures in total. Finally, on 20 November 1739 at Somerset House, before a gathering of distinguished supporters, Coram presented a Royal Charter, signed by King George II, to the Duke of Bedford for the incorporation of the Foundling Hospital. Coram was now 70 years old.

Setting up the Hospital

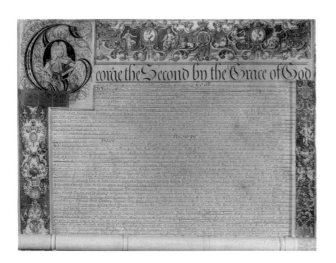

In order to ensure the Hospital's success, the Duke of Bedford was made its first President, while the Board of 172 Governors were chosen for their wealth and influence. They were aged between 21 and 80 years old and were all men – the first female Governor would not be appointed until 1921. Significantly, the only members of the Church to be invited were the Archbishops of Canterbury and York and the Bishop of London, by dint of their offices. Otherwise, the management of the Hospital was entirely secular.

Four days after receiving the Royal Charter, 50 Governors were chosen by ballot and appointed to a General Committee. They consisted largely of professional men – doctors, merchants and lawyers – and included the eminent physicians Richard Mead and Hans Sloane. They met for the first time on 29 November 1739, in a room above the Crown and Anchor pub on the Strand.

In the first two years of its existence, the Committee met every two weeks to plan the Hospital's fundraising and establishment. An account was opened at the Bank of England to receive legacies, while a book of subscription was established and pledges sought. Ambassadors and diplomats were asked to enquire about the structure and day-to-day running of similar institutions in Europe. Prominent members of the Royal College of Physicians were consulted as to whether the babies should be wet-nursed or fed by hand (wet-nursed); when they should be weaned (no sooner than a year); whether opiates should be used to calm children (absolutely not and immediate dismissal for any nurse found doing so). In due course it was decided that children under two months would be admitted and that they would be wet-nursed in the country, away from the diseases of the city and in contrast to the unhealthy workhouses. Wet nurses would be paid and regularly inspected, to ensure they were properly caring for the infants. Enquiries were made to influential people across the country in order to identify suitable people to nurse, board and oversee the children's care.

From the first, women were envisaged as being instrumental to the economical running of the Hospital. Minutes from 1740 state that:

... we hope we may receive the assistance of the Fair Sex, who altho' excluded by Custom

Fig. 6
The Royal Charter of the
Foundling Hospital, 1739

from the management of Publick Business, are by their natural tenderness and compassion peculiarly enabled to advise in the care and management of the Children, and they may without trouble to themselves see the Oeconomy of the Hospital, and communicate their observations to any Governor or to your Committee …

As the existing Poor Laws precluded the Governors carrying out a number of their plans, a supplementary Act of Parliament was required and granted the following year. This enabled the Governors to assure parishioners that babies being cared for in their parishes would not be drawing on their Poor Relief contributions.

In December 1740 a six-year lease was taken on a house in Hatton Garden while a permanent home was sought. It was decided that the Foundling Hospital's annual income enabled it to take in 60 children. Having made all the necessary preparations, secured staff and purchased furniture, laundry and clothing, the Governors gave public notice that:

… on Wednesday, the 25th March, at 8 o'clock at night, and from that time till the House should be full, their House will be opened for the reception of Children. … the person bringing it shall come in at the outward door, and ring the bell at the inward door, and not go way until the child be returned or notice given of its reception; but no questions whatsoever shall be asked of any person bringing a child, nor shall any servant of the Hospital presume to discover who such person is on pain of being dismissed.

On 14 March 1741 staff arrived to take up post. On the afternoon of Wednesday 25 March, the coat of arms designed by William Hogarth was erected above the entrance to the Hospital's temporary residence. That evening, the first 30 babies were admitted. In order to further guarantee the anonymity of the mothers, the entrance lights were extinguished and by midnight, all places were taken. The Committee minutes for the following day give a sense of the mothers' plight:

About Twelve o'Clock, the House being full the Porter was Order'd to give Notice of it to the Crowd who where without, who thereupon being a little troublesom One of the Govrs. went out and told them that as many Children were already taken in as Coud be made Room for in the House and that Notice shoud be given by a publick Advertisement as soon as any more Could possibly be admitted, And the Govrs observing Seven or Eight Women with Children at the Door and more amongst the Crowd desired them that they woud not Drop any of their Children in the Streets where they most probably must Perish but to take care of them till they could have an opportunity of putting them into

Fig. 7
William Hogarth, *Sketch for the Foundling Hospital Coat of Arms*, 1747

the Hospital which was hoped would be very soon ... On this Occasion the Expressions of Grief of the Women whose Children could not be admitted were Scarcely more observable than those of some of the Women who parted with their Children so that a more moving Scene can't well be imagined.

By the end of the first evening's admissions, eighteen boys and twelve girls had been accepted. On 29 March and in the presence of Coram, the Duke of Bedford, the Duke and Duchess of Richmond and the Countess of Pembroke, amongst other Governors and dignitaries, the first babies were named. Two babies had died before they could be baptised, one had arrived; 'as in the Agonies of Death thro' want of Food, too weak to Suck' the other 'as if Stupifyed with some Opiate'. Of the 136 babies who were admitted in the Hospital's first year of operation, 56 died.

Building the Foundling Hospital

The Governors continued to search for a suitable site on which to erect a purpose-built Hospital able to cater for 400 children. In 1740 an agreement was reached with the Earl of Salisbury to buy 56 acres of land for £6,500. The original price had been £7,000, but the Earl 'donated' £500 towards the asking price. The site was open pasture land north of Guilford Street, so beyond the city's unhealthy congestion. An architectural competition was held and won by Theodore Jacobsen, a gentleman architect and a Governor. Jacobsen's design was deliberately plain. As a charity supported by public donations and subscriptions, the Governors were keen to demonstrate their financial prudence. They were helped in this by a number of generous gifts in-kind towards the construction. These gifts inclined towards the public spaces where the donor's generosity and/or their skills could be displayed to best effect. So in addition to Jacobsen and the surveyor, James Horne, who donated their services for free, the decorative plasterwork in the rococo Court Room and the Chapel were the gift of plasterer William Wilton, the composer George Frideric Handel paid for the Chapel organ, architect Henry Keene designed and supplied the pulpit and Mr Wragg, His Majesty's smith, gave the altar railings.

The building's layout was simple and easy for small children to navigate. It consisted of two residential wings – one for boys and one for girls – separated by a central chapel and built around a large colonnaded courtyard, enabling the children to exercise in wet weather. The building also allowed for construction to take place in stages, as funds became available.

The foundation stone for the West Wing was laid on 16 September 1742 and in October 1745, the first children moved into the completed wing. The Chapel's construction was dependent on dedicated fundraising, since the Governors were not prepared to divert funds away from the children. George II gave £2,000 – almost half of the total cost – and work began in 1748. It was finally completed in 1753 and opened on 16 April with a special concert. Work began on the East Wing in 1749 at the insistence of Thomas Emerson, a Governor, who was keen to see the girls and boys given separate accommodation. Emerson would subsequently bequeath his estate to the Hospital, amounting to almost £12,000 (around two million pounds today) [see page 57]. The East Wing was completed in 1752 and each wing housed 192 children sleeping two in a bed. By the start of the 1750s, the Hospital was caring for around 600 children, including those being nursed outside London.

Fundraising and the Role of Artists

As a charity, the Foundling Hospital was in constant need of money and like all new charities, it needed to establish its profile in the public's imagination.

Coram was very fortunate in his friends and supporters. They included not only the wealthy and well connected, but also some of the leading artists of the day. Principal among these supporters were the painter and engraver William Hogarth (1697-1764) and the composer George Frideric Handel (1685-1759).

Hogarth was an early supporter of Coram's scheme and is described as a 'Governor and Guardian' in the Charter. Hogarth's childhood had been financially precarious; his father had spent five years in the Fleet Prison for bankruptcy. So he had first-hand experience of how harsh life could be and how easy it was for families to come to grief. In addition to being a Governor of the Foundling Hospital, Hogarth was also a Governor of two other hospitals; St Bartholomew's and Bethlem (Bedlam).

Hogarth was a very active Governor. He was present at Somerset House when the Royal Charter was presented, at the General Committee Meeting on the day of the first admissions, and two days later, to hear the fate of the most sickly babies. The names of both Hogarth and his wife Jane were used early on in the re-naming of the children, and as a childless couple, they subsequently fostered a number of foundlings. Hogarth designed the Hospital's coat of arms and the headpiece for the subscription roll, and it is thought he designed the children's uniforms and the decorative scheme in the Court Room. Most important of all, he donated the first artwork to the Hospital – his magnificent portrait of Thomas Coram – and encouraged all the leading artists of the day to follow suit. In this way, the Hospital

Fig. 8
Thomas Cook (1744-1818),
Gulielmus Hogarth, 1801

Fig. 9
[School of] Thomas Hudson,
George Frideric Handel, c.1737

became England's first public art gallery and established itself as a 'destination venue' for fashionable Londoners.

Although Handel came later to the cause, he quickly became invaluable to the Hospital's fundraising efforts. His involvement was not without precedent; Antonio Vivaldi had been concert master in the 1730s to the *Pieta* orphanage in Venice, successfully attracting visitors to the charity. Handel would also have known the orphanage in his home town of Halle, Germany, established in 1698 by the Lutheran pastor and philanthropist, August Herman Francke. Initially Handel offered to conduct a benefit concert in May 1749 in aid of the Chapel's completion. Handel's mixed programme included the first performance of his Foundling Hospital anthem, plus his *Music for the Royal Fireworks, Anthem on the Peace*, and excerpts from *Solomon*. The audience included the Prince and Princess of Wales and 'a great number of persons of quality and distinction' according to *The Gentleman's Magazine*. Tickets were half a guinea and over 1,000 people attended. The following year, having by this time donated the organ, Handel conducted the first benefit concert of *Messiah* in the Chapel. The event was so oversubscribed that influential supporters had to be turned away. To alleviate embarrassment and mollify disgruntled patrons, Handel repeated the performance two weeks later. He was subsequently made a Governor and concerts of *Messiah* became annual events, with Handel conducting or attending every performance. One performance alone raised 925 guineas and collectively his concerts raised the huge sum of £7,000 (over a million pounds today). Handel left a fair copy of the score and orchestral parts of *Messiah* to the Hospital in his will, so that the charity could continue to benefit from the concerts after his death.

The generosity and creative philanthropy of Hogarth, Handel and their contemporaries was remarkable. However, their support was not without a degree of professional self-interest. Both Hogarth and Handel were pioneers in their respective fields and both needed platforms on which to promote their work. This was particularly true for painters like Hogarth, who had to overcome an established prejudice against British artists. Since the Reformation, foreign artists such as Holbein, Van Dyck and Kneller had dominated British art. In the eighteenth century the situation was exacerbated by aristocratic young men undertaking the Grand Tour, which fuelled the fashion for French and Italian art. In addition to being fiercely patriotic, Hogarth was running London's only art school, the St Martin's Lane Academy. He was therefore on the lookout for ways to promote his work and that of his fellow tutors and pupils. A major new public building like the Hospital, with its influential patrons and visitors, fitted the bill perfectly.

Artists who donated work to the Hospital were made Governors. By the end of 1746, artist-Governors included Hogarth, Francis Hayman, Joseph Highmore, Thomas Hudson, George Lambert, Peter Monamy, George Moser, Allan Ramsay, James Wills, Richard Wilson, Samuel Wale and John Michael Rysbrack. Curiously, the only artist who was not made a Governor was Thomas Gainsborough, perhaps as a result of his youth. Hogarth instituted an annual dinner on 5 November at which the artist-Governors met 'to consider of what further ornaments may be added to this Hospital, without any expense to the Charity.' Since the artist-Governors numbered almost all the leading artists

of the day, these annual meetings became a forum for wider discussion about the promotion of the arts, including the establishment of a society along the lines of the European academies of painting and sculpture. Ultimately, this led to the founding of the Royal Academy of Arts in 1768.

Over the years artists continued to support the Hospital. In the nineteenth century Charles Dickens (1812-1870) became a supporter and, in the tradition of his forebears, he found his own way of helping the cause. Between 1837 and 1839 Dickens lived around the corner at 48 Doughty Street with his young family. During this time he sponsored a pew in the Chapel, sitting near the Hospital's Secretary, John Brownlow, who was himself a foundling [see page 94]. We also know of at least one mother whose petition he endorsed, Susan Mayne. Interestingly, despite his fame and influence, the Governors refused to admit Susan's baby, because her moral character was deemed insufficiently worthy. Dickens also supported the Hospital as a journalist and author. In the 19 March 1853 issue of *Household Words*, his article *Received, A Blank Child* gave a positive account of life inside the institution, while the success of novels like *Little Dorrit* and his play *No Thoroughfare*, which he co-authored with Wilkie Collins, raised the Hospital's profile internationally.

Despite the support of the great and the good, fundraising would always be a challenge. In addition to subscriptions and donations, at various points during the eighteenth century the Hospital accepted children in return for fees from parishes, from the War Office and from donations accompanying a child. The Hospital set up a rope yard in the Colonnades and the Society of Free British Fishery bought the rope, twine and nets made by the children. Money was also made from taking in needlework and from selling items made by the children such as purses and garters – so much so that Covent Garden tradesmen began to sell fakes, before the Hospital announced

Fig. 10
John Bluck (fl. 1791-1819),
Foundling Hospital, The Chapel,
1808

that foundling products could only be purchased on site. In 1773 Sub-Committee minutes state that the price of 'fine shirts fully trimm'd' was two shillings, while a large table cloth or twelve handkerchiefs fetched four pence. By 1800 proceeds from the girls' needlework stood at £174 15s 6d.

The Hospital's finances suffered huge damage following the period of General Reception [see page 21]. Not only were funds exhausted, but the public's sympathy and confidence in the institution were severely knocked. Subscriptions fell and despite every effort to reduce expenses by 1771 the Hospital was £11,000 poorer than it had been prior to General Reception. The direct result was that annual admissions dropped from around 120 children to ten. The Governors therefore reluctantly agreed to build on the land around the Hospital, in order to raise money from rents and leases. Architect Samuel Pepys Cockerell submitted his plans in 1790 for a range of residential housing and two grand squares flanking the Hospital; Brunswick Square and Mecklenburgh Square. Building was quickly underway. However, by the middle of the nineteenth century the area, including the two squares, was frequented by prostitutes and the estate mews were also becoming slums. A programme of demolition began in the 1870s and some land was sold to the Peabody Trust. Then in the 1920s both the University of London and Great Ormond Street Hospital tried to buy the site, before it was eventually sold in 1926 to a property developer, James White, for £1.65 million.

Admission Procedures in the Eighteenth Century: The Tokens

When the Hospital first opened its doors, babies were refused admission if the Chief Nurse and the Apothecary felt they had 'the French Pox, Evil, Leprosy or Disease of the like Nature'. Infectious diseases like smallpox, typhus and cholera took a devastating toll on the population and every effort was taken to protect the children. If they passed their medical examination, the Steward immediately entered the baby's details on a sheet or 'billet'. This included their sex, age, the date and hour of admission, description of the child including any identifying marks, their dress and 'particular mention is to be made of any writing, or other thing, brought with the Child'. The billet and child were then given a unique admission number which was worn around the baby's neck at all times. The baby was then dressed in new clothes, given a new name and baptised the following Sunday, before being sent to be wet-nursed in the country. Once a baby was re-named, its admission number was the only link to its origins. So this number was vitally important and quoted in reference to the child throughout its life at the Hospital.

Fig. 11
Foundling Hospital identity
disc for Bob Usherwood,
admitted 1933

You were baptised into the Foundling Hospital and given a number ... mine is 24,388, and given your foundling name ... The story goes that we were named alphabetically, or they would look in the obituaries column of the newspaper and take a Christian name and a surname and put them together ... We had the ID tag ... you were only allowed to take it off when you bathed ... We wore them for a long time, till everybody knew who was who ...

Pamela McMurtry, former pupil

From the beginning, mothers were asked to 'affix on each child some particular writing, or other distinguishing mark or token, so that the children may be known thereafter if necessary'. Further emphasis was given to the importance of tokens in 1745 and again in 1756, when it was stressed that they would be treated with the utmost care. This was because these usually mundane, but always highly personal objects provided an additional safeguard to accurately identifying a re-named foundling, should a parent ever be in a position to claim their child. Equally, if a mother was accused of infanticide – a crime punishable by death – she could prove her innocence.

On admission it was usual for a swatch of fabric to be cut from the baby's clothes. A piece was given to the mother, and the matching half attached to the billet [see pp. 35, 43, 49, 59, 77, 91]. By keeping the swatch and remembering the date her baby was admitted, a mother could provide the Hospital with the information they needed to find the relevant billet, discover the unique admission number, identify the name by which the child was now known and discover its whereabouts. However, in the event that the little piece of fabric got lost or the date of admission was forgotten, it was far more likely parents or surviving relatives would remember the unique token that was left behind, be that an item of jewellery, a piece of embroidery, or a customised penny. Until 1764, relatives reclaiming their children had to pay the cost to date of the infant's care. Once this demand ended, three or four children a year were reclaimed.

The custom of leaving tokens with babies lasted until the 1760s, when the system of admission changed and receipts were introduced. However, the custom was so established that babies were received with tokens after that date. By 1790, over 18,000 tokens had been left.

I was taken up to the Picture Gallery and ... Mr Nichols, the school Secretary wanted to see me before I went into hospital ... beside the pictures on the wall were two or three showcases ... there was nothing to say what it was, but I knew instantly what it was. There was all little tokens in there ... bits of ribbon, bits of lace, buttons, bits of material, bits of tickets, coins ... I knew instantly that these were things that ... mothers had left to be able to identify their child

Fig. 12
James II shilling, token for Elizabeth Harris, engraved 1756

by ... I suppose they all hoped at some stage ... I was just transfixed by this ... I kept wondering what my mother had left with me. Not realising, at that stage, that that system had finished years before ... It was just a heart-breaking moment.
Robert Cox, former pupil

Changes in Admission Procedures

In the early years of the Hospital, the number of foundlings admitted each year was roughly 100. However, throughout the Foundling Hospital's existence, the rules governing how children were admitted changed. Demand was always greater than the number of places available, so the Governors sought to find methods of selection that were fair. Amendments to admission rules also reflect changing attitudes to the Hospital's social function and to illegitimacy.

The Lottery System 1742-1755

Fig. 13
Nathaniel Parr after Samuel Wale (1723-1760), *An Exact Representation of the Form and Manner In Which Exposed and Deserted Young Children Are Admitted Into the Foundling Hospital*, 1749

In December 1742 in response to the Hospital's ongoing need for funds, the Committee agreed that a baby would gain automatic admission with the contribution of £100.

By 1742 admission days frequently had over 100 babies arriving for only 20 places.

Unsurprisingly, the mothers' desperation meant that the process often became unruly, which reflected badly on the Hospital. The Committee therefore decided on a lottery system which they felt was more controllable. Women would come with their babies and sit on benches, under strict instruction not to move from their seats. When it was their turn they would draw a ball from a bag and the colour of the ball would determine the fate of their baby. If the ball was white, the baby had a place if it passed its medical examination. If the ball was black, the mother and baby had to leave immediately. If a mother drew a red ball, she was taken to one side and if any of the 'white ball' babies failed to be admitted, she had the chance to draw lots again for a place. If a mother, for reasons of modesty, did not wish to be seen, she could draw her lot in a separate room or the Matron could draw it for her. For each admission, the Governors included the same number of white balls as they had places.

General Reception 1756-1760

In 1756 the most difficult period in the Foundling Hospital's admissions history began. The Hospital had received in total 1,384 children by March of that year and had roughly 600 pupils on site. The Governors were well aware that this was a drop in the ocean compared to the numbers of children in need, but the Hospital's finances could manage no more. So the Committee decided to petition Parliament for funding. Huge casualties were being sustained in the war with France, infant mortality was at an all time high, the Foundling Hospital's reputation was good and many Governors were MPs, so expectations were high for a favourable outcome. In the end, Parliament did agree to fund the Hospital to the tune of £10,000, but on condition that every baby arriving between 1 June and 31 December was accepted. The Governors made the best provision they could for the predicted onslaught. Extra staff were employed from as far afield as Yorkshire, including 60 wet nurses and 20 dry nurses for the Hospital, a night watchman, an additional porter and infirmary staff. As a precaution, the High-Constable of Holborn and 'a proper number of constables' were asked to attend the first day of General Reception.

On 2 June 1756 a basket was hung on the gate of the Hospital into which mothers, having first rung the bell and informed the Porter, could leave their babies. 425 babies were received in June – 117 on the first day alone – and all under the upper age limit of two months old. The financial impact of this influx was immediately apparent. On 30 June the Governors ruled that if a child aged over two months and under two years came with a donation of £100, they would be admitted. This remained the case until 1801.

Fig. 14
Henry Nelson O'Neil (1817-1880), *A Mother Depositing Her Child at the Foundling Hospital in Paris*, c.1855

1,783 babies were admitted between June and December 1756 and the consequences were disastrous for all concerned. Mortality rates soared from 30% to 70%, as sickly babies brought infectious diseases into the Hospital. Many babies arrived barely alive, their parents looking to avoid burial costs. Six branch hospitals in Ackworth, Aylesbury, Barnet, Chester, Shrewsbury and Westerham were opened to cope with numbers. Yet even with these, demand could not be met. Opening up admission to babies outside London enabled parishes to offload children from their workhouses. It also gave rise to a grim trade in child trafficking. Unscrupulous individuals would offer to transport babies from the countryside to London for a fee. Needless to say, some babies never arrived, dying from neglect or abandonment en route.

General Reception came to an end in 1760, by which time almost 15,000 children had been admitted and 10,389 had died in infancy, at a cost of around £500,000.

1763-1801

With the exception of the orphans of soldiers killed in active service, no babies were admitted again until 1763. When admissions restarted, the lottery system was not resumed. Instead the mother had to give her name and explain why she was unable to look after her child. Reasons included women who were married but had been deserted, widows and in one rare case, a lodging-house keeper whose guest had left without taking their baby with them. It was the beginning of a process that saw the mother's moral character brought into the process of admission.

In 1772 a system of giving receipts to mothers for their children to aid their reclamation was begun, which continued until the 1940s.

In 1795 the mother's moral character and behaviour became an explicit part of the decision-making process. The Hospital now stated that in accepting children its aim was 'restoration of the mother to work and a life of virtue'. Women's petitions speak of abandonment by unfaithful men, seduction under the promise of marriage, and rape. Many acknowledge that disgrace and unemployment await them if their babies are not accepted, even as they write of their heartbreak.

1801-1953

Finally, in 1801 illegitimacy became a requirement for admission to the Hospital, with the exception of the orphans of soldiers and sailors. Minutes from 18 February 1807 state:

... in addition to the protection of the Child, they had an opportunity of saving the Mother from shame, and of enabling her to return to her proper Situation in life, which the acknowledgement of an illegitimate Child would prevent her from doing; and that they thereby effected a double benefit, which could not be done, in the case in which the Mother was dead.

From May 1819 and for reasons that are not clear, petitioners had to state whether 'the child is of colour'. Little is known about the ethnicity of the children in the eighteenth century. References to skin colour tend to be oblique and seem to be a point of reference for identification, along with birthmarks and physical impairments. There are a few instances where babies are referred to as 'black', 'mulatto', 'negro' or 'like a Moor'. However, Britain's global expansion and its trading activities in the East and West Indies meant that a child's place of birth did not necessarily indicate its ethnic origins. Equally, there does not seem to be any correlation between a baby's skin colour and whether or not they were given surnames like Africa or Asia. Conversely, a 'mulotta Boy, with Black Hair' who was admitted to the Hospital in March 1755 was baptised Henry Agincourt.

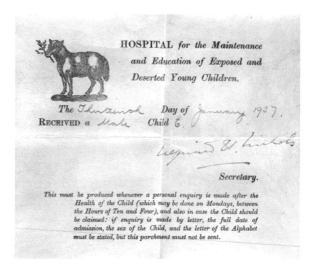

In 1836 a Government commission reported that mothers petitioning the Hospital were required to prove that the baby was illegitimate, under a year old and that she had 'borne a good character previous to her misfortune or delivery'. Furthermore in outlining the most deserving recipient of charity the writer reveals the social mores of the time:

The most meritorious case ... would be one in which a young woman, having no means of subsistence, except those derived from her own labour, and having no opulent relations, previously to committing the offence bore an irreproachable character, but yielded to artful and long-continued seduction and an express promise of marriage; whose delivery took place in secret, and whose shame was known only to one or two persons; as, for example, the medical attendant and a single relation; and, lastly whose employers and other persons were able and desirous to take her into their service, if enabled again to earn her livelihood by the reception of the child.

In 1853 the criteria were given further publicity by the most famous author of the day, Charles Dickens, who wrote about them in his article on the Hospital, *Received, A Blank Child*:

No petition is allowed to be issued, except from the porter's lodge; no previous communication with any officer of the Hospital must have been held by the mother;

Fig. 15
Receipt for the acceptance of a child into the care of the Foundling Hospital, 1937

the child must have been the first-born, and preference is given to cases in which some promise of marriage has been made to the mother, or some other deception practiced upon her. She must never have lived with the father. The object of these restrictions (careful personal inquiry being made into all such points) is as much to effect the restoration of the mother to society as to provide for her child.

These guidelines remained in place until the Hospital closed its doors as a residential institution in 1954. However, the stigma of illegitimacy lasted late into the twentieth century. In 1953 former pupils successfully achieved the right to a short form birth certificate, which removed the moral labelling inherent in their Foundling Hospital birth certificates.

One of the biggest shames was when I came to do my 'O' levels at Watford Grammar school and we had to bring in our birth certificates. And it hadn't occurred to me - I'd this big, white piece of paper that had the Foundling Hospital crest on the top - Foundling Hospital stamped right across it. 'Mother, Father: unknown.' And I had to take that in! We're all crowded round the teacher's desk and ... I was horrified ... that there it was!
Ruth Miller, former pupil

When I was 19 and I had my new birth certificate, I made an appointment to go and see [the matron at the Chelsea Hospital], ... I said 'As from today, my name is no longer Constance Millard. It's Patricia Luard.' ... She said 'Nurse Millard, hasn't anybody ever told you, you can't change your name overnight?' I said 'Well, you go and tell that to the Foundling Hospital' ... And do you know, my strong character came out the day I met my mother.
Constance Millard, former pupil

Caring for the Children

Fig. 16
Foundling Hospital birth certificate for Frank Butterworth, 1934

Around the age of five, children left their foster families and returned to the Hospital where they remained until they were apprenticed. There is no doubt that under the guardianship of the Hospital, foundling children were given a better start in life than they would otherwise have had. Great attention was given to ensuring they received better than adequate and in some cases exceptional care, with regard to health, clothing, food and education. However, life for a foundling pupil was marked by routine, anonymity and a lack of affection. It wasn't until the second half of the twentieth century that the impact of separation and loss on a child's emotional development was properly understood. The lack of maternal love and family; the knowledge of being unwanted and/or illegitimate; the wrench of leaving foster care for institutional life within the Hospital; and the constant exhortation to be grateful and obedient, must have made foundling childhoods particularly hard.

I was considered bright, but I was considered a naughty girl. But I have felt many, many times, particularly since I've been grown up, that ... really I was probably just a spirited child ... And when you're a foundling child you did not have spirit. They did not like that, they liked everybody to be the same.
Lydia Carmichael, former pupil

Health

In the eighteenth century, Hospital records show that the majority of foundlings died in the first twelve months of life. If a child survived its first two years, life expectancy rose significantly. The big threats were smallpox, measles, dysentery, whooping cough and scarlet fever. Less serious but still unpleasant were conditions such as scrofula and scabies.

Throughout its history, the Hospital benefited from having eminent physicians as Governors. Men like William Cadogan, Richard Mead and Hans Sloane established many forward-thinking practices that benefited the foundlings, such as breast-feeding, loose clothing for babies, fresh air and exercise, cleanliness and destroying the clothes of infectious children. The Hospital had an apothecary and an infirmary away from the main site. However, looking after a large number of babies in London was neither practical nor desirable, so nurses were sought in the counties around London. Each district was overseen by an Inspector – usually the local squire, parson or doctor – who had responsibility for monitoring the care of the children, buying clothing if necessary and paying the nurses and any medical expenses.

Having been admitted and baptised at the Hospital, a baby was immediately given to its nurse who travelled with it to the country. Each baby went with a comprehensive bundle of clothes, a receipt and an identification tag which was not to be removed. At the end of the first year, nurses received a premium if their baby was still alive and, from 1757, an additional payment if they cared for a baby with smallpox. If a nurse had two babies die in her care, she was not used again. All nurses, staff and residents at the Hospital had to have survived smallpox and from 1743, foundlings were inoculated against the disease on their arrival back from the country. This was done off-site to prevent 'uneasiness' among the Hospital's neighbours and in the face of 'astonishing prejudice ... among poor people'.

It seems that the majority of children were well looked after by their nurses. Many developed a strong attachment to their foster parents, calling them 'mother' and 'father'. Committee minutes make reference to apprentices running away to their foster families and some foster parents requesting their charges stay – which was rarely permitted.

My foster mother was the loveliest person … I've ever known. My foster mum spoilt me something rotten, I know some of the children at school had terrible foster parents but mine was fantastic, she spoilt me.
Sam Richardson, former pupil

It was just a job for her … we didn't have very pleasant memories of the time we were there. She would wallop us … with a stick, at the drop of a hat … So we learned at an early age just not to upset the old dear. There was never any cuddles … I never had any sort of feelings of warmth about her. But we got through.
Robert Kennison, former pupil

Recognising the emotional upheaval caused by removing five-year-olds from their nurses, the Governors allowed foundlings returning to the Hospital to play for the first few days, rather than attend classes and do chores. Also, in the first year, the boys stayed in the girls' wing in an infants' class.

I was dressed in my best and handed my teddy and my doll and the coach came to the cottage door and I climbed on board with my foster mother and we set off for Berkhamsted, which in those days was a long journey. And as we got further from home and nearer to school I asked the question: 'Will I be able to come home for my dinner?' And she said 'no' but didn't enlarge on it, and almost as we got into the school gates I said: 'I will be able to come tonight, won't I?' And as we got off the coach the boys were shepherded one way, the girls the other. And she said: 'Be a good girl' and she kissed me and she was gone.
Ruth Miller, former pupil

From early on, clear rules were laid down about bedtimes, daily routines, meals and clothing. At the Hospital foundlings wore simple, sturdy uniforms of brown serge which were communal. These were still being worn on Sundays in the 1950s. The clothes emphasised poverty and humility, and their appearance strongly hinted at the children's future careers: military for the boys, domestic service for the girls. Children were given new clothes once a year and a set of clothes at the start of their apprenticeships. The uniforms meant the children were warmly and well attired. However, like the daily routine, the uniforms denied the children a sense of individuality, reinforced their obedience and further prepared them for a life of social usefulness.

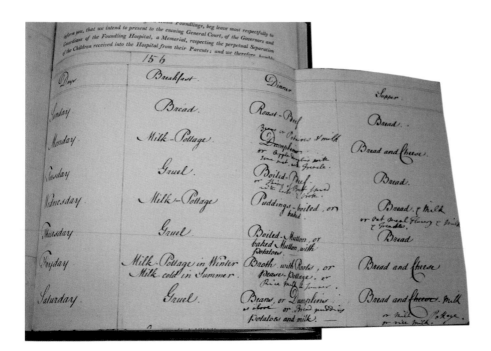

We were ... taken into the infants' dormitories ... and we had to take everything off and they took all the clothes and took them away. And then we were marched back down into the bathrooms ... and you got two kids in each and ... they scrubbed us, you know, cleaned us right up and then you were taken back, dried off, taken back into the dormitory and you were given a pair of pants and a shirt and a vest, pair of socks and a little pair of shorts and a shirt ... that was your uniform.

Joseph Deverell, former pupil

Food

Although the children's diet was repetitive, it was significantly better than that of other poor children. Weekly meals included meat, potatoes, dairy and bread, although no fish or eggs. The Governors put great efforts into ensuring the freshness and quality of the food, even during times of war when certain staples were hard to come by. Nevertheless, insufficient fresh fruit and vegetables meant that scurvy, rickets and poor eyesight were common, while limited protein meant that foundlings were often below average height. From 1747 the children were given a holiday and roast beef and plum pudding for dinner on the anniversary of the presentation of the Royal Charter. Former pupils still celebrate Charter Day each year with a lunch in the Museum's Picture Gallery.

Fig. 17
Weekly diet chart, eighteenth century

Fig. 18
Boys marching out of the
London Foundling Hospital on
the last day, 1926

Schooling

Fig. 19
Girls in the schoolroom in the
London Foundling Hospital

In order to study the Bible, the children were taught to read. They also learnt practical skills like spinning, weaving and needlework, including repairing uniforms, knitting gloves and darning. Initially the children were not taught to write, as this was felt to be unnecessary and liable to give them ideas above their station. However, in 1757 the first professional teachers were employed, including the pioneering Mr Redpath. Shortly thereafter the boys and girls were taught to read and write. Coram had championed educating girls, arguing that it was essential if they were to be good mothers. This may explain why foundling girls received such an unusually high standard of education for the time, which would later include bookkeeping. By the end of the eighteenth century some of the boys were learning arithmetic – useful for an apprentice tradesman – and most left able to write. This compared favourably with the general population, where only 40% of men could sign their names. By the mid-nineteenth century boys and girls were being taught reading and writing, grammar, mathematics and geography. In the twentieth century the education was broadened still further.

Musical Education

One aspect of the Hospital's education that marked it out from other charity schools was its music. As early as 1774, there were discussions about teaching music at the Hospital. Despite support from influential Governors and advice from the composer and violinist Felice de Giardini, it was felt that music was a luxury inappropriate to the status of the children. So initially it was only blind children like Tom Grenville, Blanch Thetford, John Printer and Jane Freer who were taught the organ and singing, in order to perform in the Chapel. From the 1760s choral singing began to be taught more generally. Before long the Governors realised that children with musical talent could support the Hospital's fundraising. In 1771 they resolved to employ someone to determine the musical talents of the children and instruct up to 20 of them. The blind musician and composer John Stanley (1712-1786) was a Governor. He wrote hymns and anthems for the Hospital, conducted benefit concerts, and supported the children's musical education. The Chapel employed a professional choir, whose members included well-known figures from the world of opera. Yet by 1850 the standard of the children's singing was so high that the Governors decided they could dispense with professional singers. By this time the boys were also being taught to play musical instruments. In 1847 John Brownlow had persuaded the Governors to start a boys' band and many boys would enter the military via the regimental bands.

... there was this thing about the Chapel, the peace, the quiet, the beautiful stained glass windows, all of this actually had a profound effect on me ... I first heard the organ playing in the Chapel, I was ... completely overwhelmed, this gigantic sound reverberating around the Chapel, to me, was absolute bliss and that was the beginning, I think, of my interest and appreciation of music.
John Caldicott, former pupil

Apprenticeships

The children were responsible for much of the Hospital's running, from dressing the younger children and cleaning, to drawing water and tending the vegetable gardens. However, the Governors sought to apprentice the children as soon as they could, usually around the age of ten. In 1806, a resolution was passed that no child was to be apprenticed under the age of fourteen. Although the Charter stipulated that boys should be apprenticed to the age of 24 and girls to the age of 21, this was the maximum age and it was unusual they lasted this long. More usually, apprenticeships were at least seven years and once completed, the young people were equipped with a trade and a means of providing for themselves and benefiting society.

The first apprenticeships began in 1751 and a sub-committee was established to manage them. All children were to be apprenticed to Protestants and on completion, they received a financial reward. Close attention was paid to the suitability of employers, with checks made on their financial situation and respectability. Contracts required that the foundlings were well fed, clothed, housed and allowed to attend church on Sunday morning. Boys tended to follow careers in the military, maritime services and trade, excepting Public Houses. The majority of girls became domestic servants. They would be apprenticed to a housekeeper and never to the home of an unmarried man.

Of the 104 girls who were apprenticed between 1751 and 1760, 73 were in domestic service and thirteen were calico printers. In the same period, of the 104 apprentice boys, 42 were in service at sea, eighteen were learning husbandry and gardening, while the others were apprenticed to butchers, cheesemongers, comb makers, bookbinders, jewellers and peruke (wig) makers. In the twentieth century, domestic service and the military were still common career paths for pupils.

The Governors followed the progress of the apprenticeships with inspections and written reports. Ill treatment would result in the children being removed and, in some cases, the employers being prosecuted. Very occasionally there were instances of appalling neglect and abuse, which resulted in the death of apprentices; but in the main, the system worked well. While it was rare for a foundling to reach a position of eminence, most were able to make a living as a result of their training. Disabled children tended to remain at the Hospital. Some became known for their skill at needlework and music, and all seem to have been cared for until the end of their lives.

The Twentieth Century

By 1926 the Hospital was no longer an oasis from the disease and pollution of the city; it had been subsumed into central London. The decision was made to sell the site, which resulted in the Jacobsen building being torn down. The children were moved temporarily to premises in Redhill, before taking up residence in a purpose-built school in Berkhamsted, Hertfordshire, designed by John Sheppard. The Governors subsequently bought back a plot of land in the north-west corner of the Hospital's original site. Here, at 40 Brunswick Square, Sheppard built a London headquarters, incorporating elements of Jacobsen's building, which opened in 1938. Today it is the Foundling Museum, but until the 1990s it was still the place at which mothers would leave their babies. As such, the building has particular significance for former pupils of the Foundling Hospital, many of whom describe it as their 'spiritual home.'

The systems and routines of the eighteenth and nineteenth-century Foundling Hospital remained largely unchanged at Berkhamsted. The children's education improved and broadened, particularly for girls, but military and domestic service remained the principal careers for Foundling boys and girls.

... bandmasters from regular Army units would ... turn up by appointment, go down to the Band School, have a word with our School bandmaster and see which boys ... they thought were appropriate for their band. You had no choice. You didn't speak to the bandmaster visiting. Our School bandmaster would presumably say, 'He's suitable', 'He's not' ... you then were earmarked for that band. You didn't know which band, which regiment, you didn't know anything.
Sidney Ansell, former pupil

After the Second World War, attitudes towards children's emotional needs changed. The children's biological mothers were encouraged to maintain contact, foster families remained in touch with their Foundling children and by the early 1950s, the benefits of fostering in the community rather than institutionalising children were being recognised by society at large. In 1953 the Hospital ceased to have children 'living in' and the Berkhamsted building passed to the control of the local authority. Today it exists as Ashlyns School. The charity became the Thomas Coram Foundation for Children, offering a range of nursery, welfare and foster services. By 1974 the Coram Children's Centre at 49 Mecklenburgh Square was pioneering an integrated approach to the care of children. Today, the charity exists as Coram and is a leader in the field of adoption services [see page 92].

Fig. 20
Enamel token marked Ann Higs, eighteenth century

John Bowles: Baby 5

The first babies to be admitted to the Foundling Hospital's temporary home at Hatton Garden arrived on 25 March 1741. They included a baby boy who was dressed in a brown cloak and a 'clout' or nappy. Registered as baby number 5, he was named John Bowles and sent to his nurse in the country on 13 April. Of the 30 children taken in on that first admission, only six survived to apprenticeship – four boys and two girls – and John was the first to be apprenticed.

By the time John returned from the country on 24 May 1746, the new purpose-built Hospital had been opened. In July he contracted measles and on 30 October he was inoculated with smallpox. This meant his value as an apprentice would be higher, since he would not contract the disease in the future.

On 7 August 1751 John was bound apprentice to Stephen Beckingham Esq. and 'went down with him to Barham in Kent' (Bourne Place, near Canterbury). His trade is not stated but he was probably taken on as a gardener or general servant. Sir Stephen Beckingham (1693–1752) married Lady Mary Cox in 1729 and their wedding was painted by William Hogarth. His son, also called Stephen Beckingham (1729-1813), was a Hospital Governor for some years and when Captain Thomas Coram died in 1751, Stephen Beckingham is listed as one of the Governors who carried the pall at the funeral service. It is possible that Sir Stephen first apprenticed John, but the apprenticeship was continued by his son when he inherited his father's estate.

Bourne Place was later the home of Horace Mann, the nephew of the diplomat Sir Horace Mann who lived in Florence, Italy. When the Governors were first setting up the Foundling Hospital they wrote to Sir Horace to ask how the system worked in Florence's *Ospedale degli Innocenti*. In July 1765 the eight-year-old Mozart and his family stayed for a month at Bourne Place, breaking their journey between London and Dover.

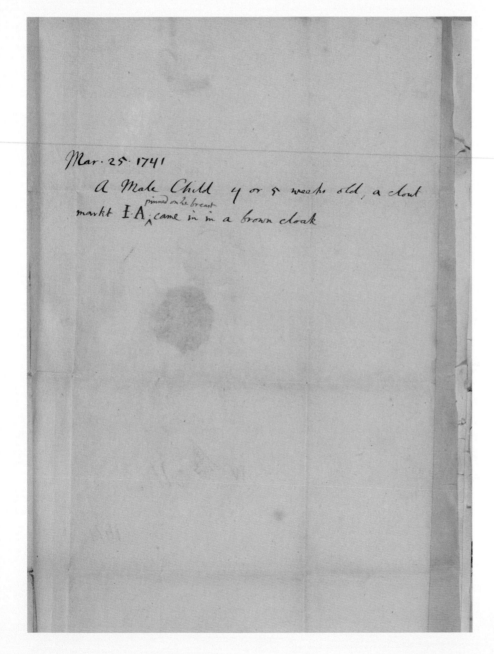

Mar. 25. 1741

A Male Child 4 or 5 weeks old, a clout
markt I·A, came in in a brown cloak
pinned on he breast

Fig. 21
Billet book page for John
Bowles, Baby 5, admitted as
part of the first intake on 25
March 1741

COMMITTEE ROOM

This room is an accurate reconstruction of one of the original Hospital interiors. Many paintings in this room reference daily life at the Hospital.

In the centre of the room is a seventeenth-century refectory table. Judging by the wear on its surface, the table is likely to have come from the kitchen. The chimneypiece and overmantel are from the original building and are thought to have been designed by Hogarth. Contained within the chimney breast is a painting by George Lambert (1700-1765), *Landscape with Figures*. Lambert was a pioneer of landscape painting in England, as well as a well-known scene-painter for the theatre manager John Rich (1692-1761). Rich and Lambert are both credited with founding The Sublime Society of Beef Steaks at the Theatre Royal, Covent Garden, whose members included Hogarth and the actor David Garrick. Lambert and Hogarth knew each other well, having worked together on the murals at St Bartholomew's Hospital where Hogarth was also a Governor. Although this bucolic scene is invented, in its early years of existence the Hospital was set in over fifty acres of open pasture. To the right of the fireplace is a cabinet of communion silverware; a reminder of the central place that Anglican religious education had in the children's lives.

Opposite the fireplace are a series of four paintings by Emma Brownlow (1832-1905) depicting life at the Foundling Hospital. Emma Brownlow's work is interesting for a number of reasons. Firstly, opportunities for women to study and practise oil painting in the nineteenth century were limited, making her work unusual. Secondly, Emma Brownlow grew up around foundlings as her father, John Brownlow, was the Hospital's Secretary from 1849 to 1872. So her scenes are likely to be essentially accurate, if idealised. John Brownlow was himself a foundling and by all accounts a kindly man. He corresponded with foundlings' mothers, giving them progress reports on their children; he wrote the first history of the Hospital; and there is a letter from Dickens to Brownlow in the archive. There may have been a degree of shared understanding between the two men, since Dickens had had a difficult childhood and was ashamed of his upbringing. Dickens wrote *Oliver Twist* while he was living round the corner at 48 Doughty Street. People like to believe that the kindly Mr Brownlow, who rescues Oliver from a life on the streets, is modelled on John Brownlow. However, it is more likely Dickens named the character after a nearby street. Tellingly, Emma Brownlow represents her father in *The Foundling Restored to its Mother*. The four paintings illustrate a number of aspects of life at the Hospital: the uniforms; the role that older pupils took in caring for the younger ones; the system of petitions and admissions; and the infirmary. She also depicts the Hospital's art collection *in situ*, including several works that you encounter on your travels around the Museum. In

Opposite:
Fig. 22
Detail from Emma Brownlow,
The Foundling Restored to its Mother, 1858

particular, in *The Christening* you can see *Christ Presenting a Little Child* by Benjamin West (1738-1820), [see pp 45-46] which is on the staircase, and the font which is in the Introductory Gallery. On the wall behind her father in *The Foundling Restored to its Mother* is *The March of the Guards to Finchley* by William Hogarth (1697-1764), which hangs at the end of the Committee Room. This painting recounts the successful defeat in 1745 of the Jacobite Rebellion, led by the Catholic Bonnie Prince Charlie against Protestant King George II. Hogarth depicts George's troops mustering at the Tottenham Court Turnpike and marching north to Finchley, there to set up camp and protect London from the enemy. Against this backdrop of reportage, Hogarth paints a portrait of his fellow citizens as boisterous, conflicted, unruly but ultimately admirable. The painting divides neatly down the centre. On the left is all that's good/Protestant: beer, nuclear families, rosy-cheeked children, healthy leisure pursuits (boxing), and the call to arms, all presided over by a very British Garden of Eden – the Adam & Eve pub next to the Tottenham Court Nursery and an oak tree in full leaf. On the right you have the grim/Catholic alternative: gin and gin-addicted children, prostitution and drunkenness, overseen by the notorious brothel keeper Mother Douglas, a sign of Charles II (who reverted to Catholicism on his deathbed) and a barren tree. Finally, in the centre, you have a young Grenadier guard who has a choice to make that is both personal and political. Does he go with his pregnant girlfriend, the ballad singer selling songs loyal to George II, or with the Catholic prostitute who carries Jacobite propaganda? Although his expression seems far from convinced, his step has fallen in with his girlfriend's. So like the soldiers in the distance who are marching forth in good order, it seems he will do his duty as a father and a soldier. Hogarth designed this work to be sold as a print for 7s, 6d. To prevent the original painting falling into the hands of picture dealers whom he disliked, he advertised that for an extra 3 shillings, subscribers to the print could be entered into a lottery to win the painting. 2,000 tickets were available and come the day of the draw, 157 remained unsold. As a Governor of the Hospital he generously donated the unsold tickets to the charity and un/surprisingly, the Hospital won. Having generated interest in the painting via the publicity surrounding the lottery, the public could now come and see the original and the charity's good work in action.

Fig. 23
Emma Brownlow,
The Christening, 1863

Fig. 24
George Lambert, *Landscape
with Figures*, 1757

Overleaf:
Fig. 25
Detail from William Hogarth,
*The March of the Guards to
Finchley*, 1750

Thomas Coram: Baby 38

On 17 April 1741 a baby boy was admitted with 29 other babies, as part of the Hospital's second intake of children at Hatton Garden. His billet states that he was about two months old, wearing a fine white India dimity mantle and white corded dimity sleeves 'exceeding neat', and was admitted and sent to the care of a Mrs Wilkinson. The boy also came with a letter which read:

St Andrews Holborn 17th April: 1741 / I was Born in this Parish on Tuesday 24th February last & have been Christened in the Said Church by the name of Thomas, Soe my name is Thos [Cay?] / Pray use me well and you shall find / my Father will not prove unkind / Unto that Nurse who, is my protector / Because he is a Benefactor / Wether ye Child live or die be please to Send an aco.t [account] thereof to ye Jamaica Coffee house in St Michaels alley, in one months Time Directed to M:J it will be acknowledge … great Favour.

In addition to his billet is a piece of parchment marked with the letter C. At the point of admission, children were marked with letters of the alphabet and only given a number the following day. This was to ensure that people who brought babies to the Hospital never saw a child's identification number.

On 9 April the babies were baptised by Revd Smith. A boy from the Hospital's first admission had been baptised Thomas Coram, but he had died by the time baby 38 was admitted, so the name was re-used. On 22 April six children, including Thomas Coram, were sent to nurses near Uxbridge in Middlesex, under the inspection of Mrs Blencome.

On the 8 August 1753 Henry Bird Jnr, ship builder of Surrey, approached the Hospital about taking an apprentice for sea service and 'Thomas Coram' is noted in the margin. A week later, Bird returned to ask if he could take Thomas Coram within a few days as an apprentice, as his ship was due to sail. This was agreed.

Henry Bird Jnr built many ships for the Royal Navy. One of the most famous was HMS Supply, which was launched in 1759, so it is possible that Thomas Coram worked upon it as part of his apprenticeship. Twenty-seven years later, the Supply was part of the First Fleet, eleven ships that left Portsmouth on 13 May 1787 to found a penal colony in Botany Bay, Australia.

In anecdotal records from the 1840s, the Hospital's Secretary Morris Lievesley comments that in later life this same foundling, Thomas Coram, was wealthy enough to come to Hospital concerts in his own carriage.

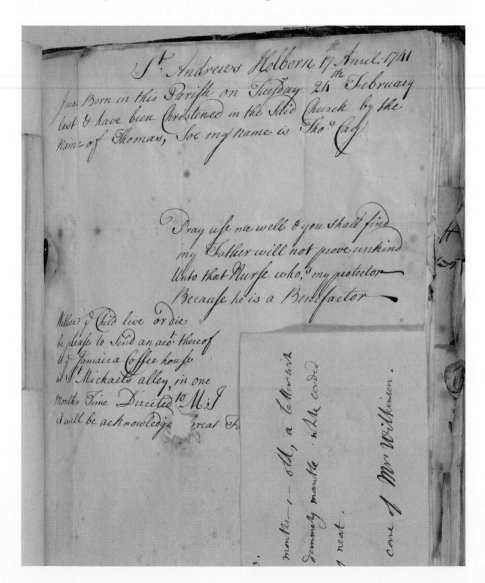

Fig. 26
Billet book page for Thomas Coram, Baby 38, admitted 17 April 1741

THE STAIRCASE

The oak staircase was originally situated in the West Wing – the boys' wing – of the Foundling Hospital. In August 1773 a boy attempted to slide down the banister and fell to his death. As a result, a spiked iron rail was added above the banister and a framed notice put on the stair. This stated that any child attempting anything similar 'shall be confined in a dark room and fed upon bread and water', receiving 'as many Lashes as the Sub-Committee judge necessary for so great an offence.' The girls' staircase was incorporated into the Foundling Hospital in Berkhamsted. Both the Berkhamsted building and 40 Brunswick Square were designed by architect John Sheppard.

Portraits of Governors line the staircase along with a number of genre scenes. Half way up the stairs is a portrait of *Mrs Patrick Forbes*, 1906, by William Carter (1863-1939). This is one of only two portraits of women in the entire Foundling Hospital Collection. Beatrice Forbes was one of the Hospital's few female Governors. Her father, Robert Grey, was Treasurer of the Foundling Hospital from 1892 to 1914 and his portrait hangs nearby. *The Pinch of Poverty* by Thomas Kennington (1856-1916) was bequeathed to the Hospital in 1926. Kennington was best known for his scenes of upper-class life and idealised domestic interiors, often involving the mother and child. This picture, however, is one of a series in which he shows the suffering caused by poverty. Others in the series are entitled *Homeless*, 1885, *Widowed and Fatherless*, 1885, and *Orphans*, 1890.

On the first floor landing are a number of items that relate to the Chapel. The *Adoration of the Magi* by Andrea Casali (1705-1784) was painted to hang above the altar, and it was installed there in 1752. However, in 1801 it was moved to the Boys' Dining Room and replaced by the more sober *Christ Presenting a Little Child* by Benjamin West, now hanging on the stairs. Neither Casali nor West were British. Casali was born in Rome and came to London in 1741, following his aristocratic Grand Tour patrons back home. His rococo style became very popular in the 1750s and he stayed in England for over 20 years before returning to Italy. West was born in Pennsylvania, America. A close friend of Benjamin Franklin, one of America's founding fathers, West's wealthy patrons enabled him to travel first to Italy, to study the Renaissance masters, and then to London, where he remained for the rest of his life. West became very successful and was best known for his dramatic, large scale history paintings. In 1772 he was made historical painter to the court of George III, before becoming Surveyor of the King's Pictures in 1791. The following year he succeeded Joshua Reynolds as President of the Royal Academy of Arts. *Christ Presenting a Little Child* was commissioned by the printseller and picture dealer, Thomas Macklin, for his seven-volume Bible. Macklin's Bible was designed to promote contemporary British

Opposite:
Fig. 27
Detail from Thomas Benjamin Kennington, *The Pinch of Poverty*, 1891

45

painting and it contained over 70 illustrations by artists including Reynolds, John Landseer and Henry Fuseli. After Macklin's death, West's painting was purchased by the Foundling Hospital Governors. West retouched the picture without charge before it was hung in the Chapel and he was subsequently made a Governor. Fourteen years later West had to retouch it again after the work had deteriorated.

The pew and two lead cartouches that hang either side of the *Adoration* are also from the Chapel. The cartouches were presented by the artist Edward Ives. The magnificent longcase clock on the landing is by John Ellicott (1706-1772), one of the leading clock-makers of the age and a fellow of the Royal Society. He presented this clock to the Hospital in 1750 and in 1757 he was made a Governor of the Hospital. Ellicott also advised on the installation of a turret clock above the Chapel, recommending William Harrison (1728-1815) for the work. Harrison was the son of John Harrison, the inventor of the marine chronometer which won the Longitude prize in 1765. Charles Dickens and Wilkie Collins would later refer to the Foundling Hospital Chapel clock in their play *No Thoroughfare*, 1867:

Day of the month and year, November the thirtieth, one thousand eight hundred and thirty-five. London Time by the great clock of Saint Paul's, ten at night. All the lesser London churches strain their metallic throats. Some, flippantly begin before the heavy bell of the great cathedral; some, tardily begin three, four, half a dozen, strokes behind it; all are in sufficiently near accord, to leave a resonance in the air, as if the winged father who devours his children, had made a sounding sweep with his gigantic scythe in flying over the city. What is this clock lower than most of the rest, and nearer to the ear, that lags so far behind to-night as to strike into the vibration alone? This is the clock of the Hospital for Foundling Children. Time was, when the Foundlings were received without question in a cradle at the gate. Time is, when inquiries are made respecting them, and they are taken as by favour from the mothers who relinquish all natural knowledge of them and claim to them for evermore.

Fig. 28
Benjamin West, *Christ Presenting a Little Child*, 1801

Opposite:
Fig. 29
Andrea Casali, *Adoration of the Magi*, 1750

Catharine Hunter: Baby 2,214

Marther Bowyers was eleven days old when she was admitted to the Foundling Hospital on 28 August 1756. Her mother lived in the parish of Spitalfields and Marther came during the period known as General Reception when, in return for government funding, all babies brought to the Hospital were admitted. This put enormous strain on the Hospital's resources, so much so that branch hospitals had to be opened across the country to cope with the influx of babies. Marther was renamed Catharine Hunter and on 5 September she was sent to a branch hospital in Ackworth, Yorkshire to be wet-nursed.

Catharine was placed in the care of Eleanor Ward, who lived in Hemsworth, just outside Ackworth. The inspector who was responsible for 50 children, including Catharine, between Hemsworth and Doncaster, was Revd Trant. After the children had been weaned, they went to a house run by Revd Trant where girls like Catharine were taught reading, sewing, knitting, spinning and netting.

In December 1761 Catharine was transferred to Ackworth Hospital. Here many children were trained for work in the wool-manufacturing trades. However, just before her twelfth birthday Catherine was apprenticed to a farmer, John Middleton, who lived in the parish of Brayton. Ordinarily, Catharine's apprenticeship would have lasted until she was 21 or until she married – whichever was sooner. We do not know whether Catharine completed her apprenticeship, but on 27 November 1791 she married John Wood in Howden Minster.

John came from Balkholme, ten miles away from Brayton, and in the marriage register he is described as a 'husbandman', a position of some authority in a farming community. John and Catharine had three children: William, John and Mary, who was born when Catharine was 44 years old. Catharine died in 1820 and was buried in Howden churchyard on 2 March.

Catharine has 83 descendants; 51 are alive today and living in the UK and Australia.

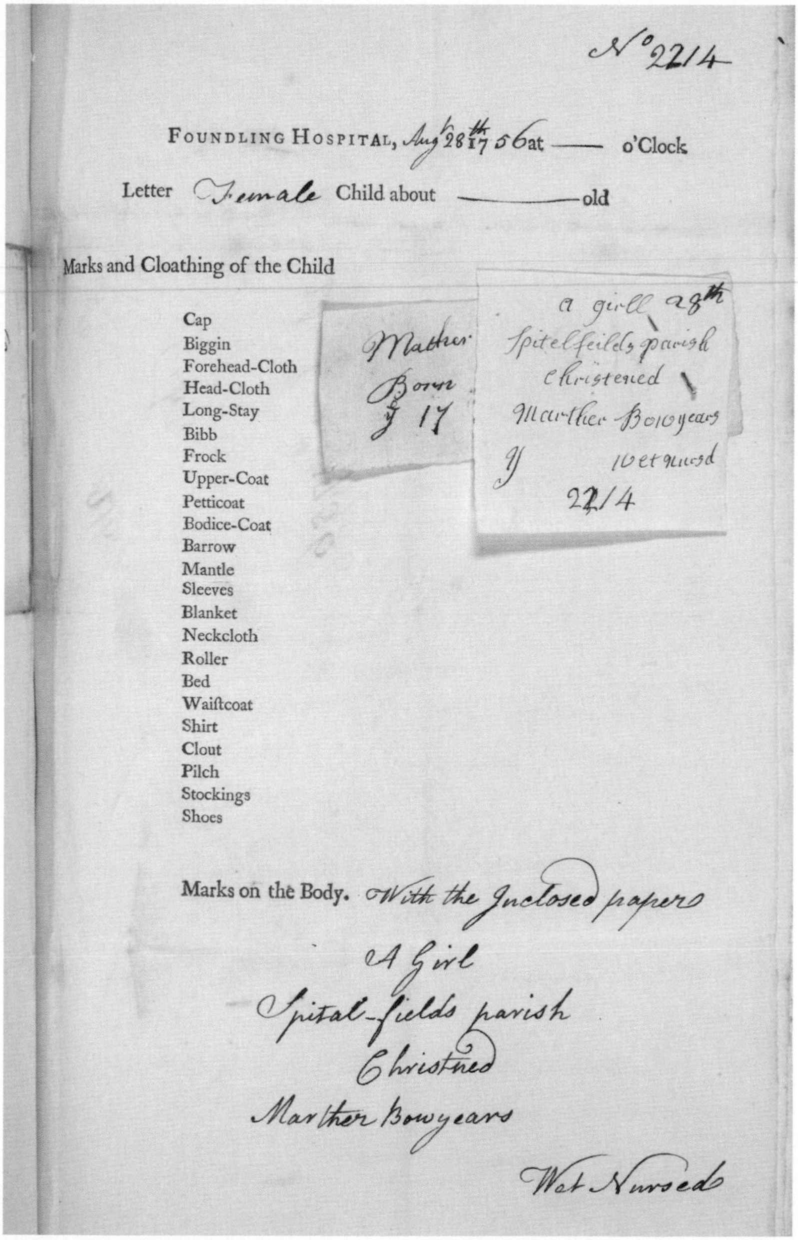

Nº 2214

FOUNDLING HOSPITAL, Augt 28th 1756 at —— o'Clock

Letter Female Child about ———— old

Marks and Cloathing of the Child

Cap
Biggin
Forehead-Cloth
Head-Cloth
Long-Stay
Bibb
Frock
Upper-Coat
Petticoat
Bodice-Coat
Barrow
Mantle
Sleeves
Blanket
Neckcloth
Roller
Bed
Waiftcoat
Shirt
Clout
Pilch
Stockings
Shoes

Mather Born y 17

a girll 28th
Spitelfeilds parish
christened
Marther Bowyears
y Wet nursd
2214

Marks on the Body. With the Inclosed papers

A Girl
Spital-fields parish
Christned
Marther Bowyears
Wet Nursed

Fig. 30
Billet book page for Catharine Hunter, Baby 2,214, admitted 28 August 1756

PICTURE GALLERY

This room is a reconstruction of the original Picture Gallery in the West Wing of the Hospital. The grandeur of the room and the quality of the art on display provided elegant surroundings in which to entertain potential supporters. The room also underlined the institution's reliance on philanthropy, since most of the portraits were of Governors and benefactors. Furthermore, many of the paintings prominently state that they were 'given' by the artist. Almost all the eighteenth-century paintings are in their original frames and many were painted by the most celebrated portraitists of the day. They provide a snapshot of the different styles of portraiture available to patrons in the mid-eighteenth century, from the baroque Grand Manner, to the softer but no less flattering rococo. Amongst the set pieces, Hogarth's singular and original image of his friend Thomas Coram stands out.

Captain Thomas Coram by Hogarth was the first work of art to be given to the Hospital – a fact prominently stated in the inscription at Coram's feet. As an artist, Hogarth gives Coram magisterial status by including all the devices common to baroque portraiture: a dramatic sunrise, heavy drapery, a classical column, a glove (the sign of a gentleman), and strategically placed objects that allude to his maritime career in America and Britain. However, as a friend, Hogarth reveals the character and qualities that made the man: a face marked by hard work and sea air, a head of white hair, the emblematic red coat rumpled from exertion, and a restless foot lifted off the floor as if in mid-movement – as well as an honest reference to Coram's lack of height. The shaft of light that falls across Coram highlights both his great and lasting achievement – the Royal Charter establishing the Hospital - and the personal toll that seventeen years of campaigning took on his health and life. Sadly, a year after this portrait was painted, Coram was removed from the Board of Governors. It seems that his plain speaking and lack of diplomacy brought him into conflict with his aristocratic colleagues. The dogged qualities that had served him so well during his campaign were less suited to flattering donors and dealing with the minutiae of running an institution. He was overlooked by all the sub-committees running the Hospital's business, but continued to attend baptisms, standing as godfather to over 20 foundlings. He would also sit in the Colonnades and distribute gingerbread to the children. Towards the end of his life Coram fell on hard times. In 1749 his friends and the financier Sampson Gideon raised a subscription which provided him with an annuity. Coram died on 29 March 1751 and was buried beneath the altar of the Hospital Chapel.

Next to Coram is the portrait of *Dr Richard Mead* painted by Allan Ramsay (1713-1784). Mead (1673-1754) was a leading clinician and physician to George II. He wrote on public health and was an early champion of smallpox inoculation – so much

so that he is reported to have fought a duel over the matter. As a founding Governor of the Hospital, his medical expertise was used to shape the healthcare of the children. Mead was also an important collector of art, antiquities and books, which were said to number over 10,000 volumes. His collections were made available to scholars at his home in Great Ormond Street. Mead was Ramsay's patron. He enabled the Scottish artist to travel to Italy in 1736 in order to study the Classical and Renaissance masters. This was considered essential if an artist was to excel in the Grand Manner. By the 1740s, Ramsay was established as a leading portrait painter and this work is a baroque masterclass in how to bestow drama and gravitas upon a physically unprepossessing sitter. It is easy to imagine that Ramsay's ego was piqued on seeing Coram's portrait painted by the self-taught Hogarth. There seems to be a hint of riposte in this work in terms of Mead's pose and his setting.

To the left of the fireplace are two full length portraits by Thomas Hudson (1701-1779) of Governors *John Milner*, 1746, and *Theodore Jacobsen*. Hudson was another fashionable portrait painter of the day, famed for his ability to flatter his sitters. His many students included Joseph Wright of Derby and Joshua Reynolds, who would ultimately eclipse his teacher. John Milner was a barrister and played a significant role in the establishment of the Hospital. He laid the foundation stone on 16 September 1742 and served as a Vice-President between 1740 and 1750. His correspondence with Hans Sloane, who was President of the Royal Society, led to the system of wet nurses and the emphasis on not weaning babies before twelve months. He also oversaw the Hospital's ballot system for admitting babies, and at Coram's death in April 1751 was one of the pallbearers at his funeral. The serious tone of Milner's portrait is absent in that of Theodore Jacobsen. Jacobsen was a gentleman architect and a member of the Royal Society, the Society of Arts and the Society of Antiquaries. In his early career he had been a merchant linked to the Steel Yard on Upper Thames Street. The Steel Yard had been the base for German and Flemish traders since the thirteenth century and Jacobsen's uncle and grandfather had both held high office there. In addition to the Foundling Hospital, Jacobsen designed the Haslar Royal Hospital for sick soldiers at Gosport. Jacobsen was a founding Governor and gave his designs free of charge. Hudson was made a Governor in 1746 and the inscription on this painting highlights that the work was gifted to the Hospital.

Over the fireplace is a portrait of *Thomas Emerson*, 1731, by Joseph Highmore (1692-1780). Emerson was a wealthy merchant and 'sugar baker', who owned sugar refineries on Thames Street and later in Battersea. He was elected a Governor of the Hospital

Fig. 32
Allan Ramsay, *Dr Richard Mead*, 1747

in 1739 and it was his insistence that the girls and boys should be separated that saw work begin on the East Wing in 1749. Like Coram, Hogarth and Handel, Emerson was childless. When he died in 1745 he left the bulk of his estate to the Hospital – some £12,000, which today would be around two million pounds. Emerson also bequeathed this portrait to the Hospital, which had hung in the great parlour of his home in Battersea. The portrait can be seen in the background of a 1749 engraving representing the admission of foundlings [see page 20]. In his will, Emerson also left annuities for his sister and a female servant, with elaborate instructions to ensure that their husbands did not use the money for their own purposes or to clear their debts. It raises an intriguing question as to which came first; his awareness of the dangers faced by women with no financial security, or his involvement with the Hospital. Highmore was the son of a coal merchant whose business, like Emerson's, was based in Thames Street. His uncle had been Sergeant Painter to Queen Anne, but having failed to be taken on as his pupil, Highmore was articled as an attorney. He later abandoned the law to become a student of Godfrey Kneller (1646-1723), the pre-eminent portraitist of the early eighteenth century. Highmore was particularly popular with the middle classes who liked the lack of pretension in his portraits and his ability to catch a likeness. He was elected a Governor in 1746.

To the left of the fireplace is a portrait of *Taylor White*, 1758, by Francis Cotes (1726-1770). Cotes was a fashionable portraitist, a pioneer of pastel painting in England and a founding member of the Royal Academy. White was the Hospital's Treasurer from 1745 to 1772, during which time he attended over 3,000 Committee meetings. A successful barrister on the Northern Circuit and subsequently a judge, White's strong connections to the north of England were probably responsible for a branch hospital being opened in Yorkshire during General Reception [see page 21]. Taylor White is also responsible for the painting on the other side of the fireplace, *A Flagship before the Wind under Easy Sail, with a Cutter, a Ketch and other Vessels*, 1754, by Charles Brooking (1723-1759). White was an admirer of Brooking's art and persuaded him to make a work for the Hospital. As Brooking's lodgings were very small, he had to paint this canvas in situ, managing to complete it in just eighteen days. This work established Brooking as one of the leading maritime painters of the day. The Foundling Hospital Collection contains a number of other fine maritime paintings, including *Action off the Coast of France, 13 May 1779*, 1779, by Thomas Luny (1759-1837) and *The Battle of Trafalgar*, 1848 by W E D Stuart (d.1858).

Facing the portrait of Coram is the portrait of *William Legge*, 1757, by Joshua Reynolds (1723-1792). Legge (1731-1801) was the second Earl of Dartmouth and a Vice President

Fig. 33
Thomas Hudson, *Theodore Jacobsen*, 1746

of the Foundling Hospital for almost 50 years. He was a member of the Cabinet and was serving as President of the Board of Trade when news of the Boston Tea Party arrived in England. Dartmouth College in New Hampshire, USA is named after him. Reynolds was one of the most successful and fashionable portrait painters of the age and went on to become the first President of the Royal Academy. Although not one of his most accomplished works, Reynolds donated this painting to the Hospital in 1757.

Opposite the fireplace are two ceramic punch bowls and a terracotta portrait bust of *George Frideric Handel*. The bust is by Louis François Roubiliac (1702-1762) and was a model for a marble version, now at Windsor Castle, which was given to George III who was a great admirer of Handel. Roubiliac was born in Lyons and came to England in about 1730. He was a friend of Hogarth and a tutor at the St Martin's Lane Academy. His reputation as one of the foremost portrait sculptors of the day was established in 1738, when he made a life-size marble sculpture of Handel for Jonathan Tyers, the manager of Vauxhall Pleasure Gardens. This sculpture (as well as a copy of his sculpture of Hogarth's dog, Trump) is in the Victoria and Albert Museum. In 1761, Roubiliac created the monument for Handel's tomb in Westminster Abbey, a model for which is on display in the Handel Gallery upstairs.

To one side of Handel's bust is a rare porcelain famille rose 'London' Punchbowl, from the second half of the eighteenth century. Made in Jingdezhen, south east China, it is decorated with scenes taken from engravings originally published in London in the 1750s. On one side is a view of the Foundling Hospital and on the other, Vauxhall Gardens. Although this seems a curious pairing, the two organisations had many connections. Hogarth and Handel were the creative brains behind the art and music at Vauxhall which, like the Hospital, promoted British culture to the public. Under Tyers' management, Vauxhall created the first mass audience for contemporary art and music in this country. Poignant proof of the Gardens' popularity lies in a 1737 copper season ticket to the Gardens, which was used by a mother as a token and left with her baby in the 1740s. The other English delftware punchbowl dates from around 1720. The blue dragon is an interpretation of a Chinese porcelain design of the Kangxi period (1662-1722). Tradition has it that this punch bowl belonged to Hogarth and was bequeathed by him or his widow to the Foundling Hospital. These two punchbowls demonstrate how the fashion for Chinese ceramics was catered for at both ends of the market, from relatively cheap, domestic, earthenware imitations, to valuable porcelain 'originals', made specifically for export.

The portrait of *George II*, 1758, is by John Shackleton (fl. 1749-1767), who made many versions of his portrait of the King. George II granted the Royal Charter establishing the Foundling Hospital in 1739 and also donated £2,000 towards the construction of the Chapel. In 1758 he became the Hospital's patron. Shackleton was made Principal

Opposite:
Fig. 34
Louis François Roubiliac,
George Frideric Handel, 1739

Painter in Ordinary to George II in 1749, an honour that was also bestowed upon Allan Ramsay and Joshua Reynolds. He was elected a Governor in 1758, the year he presented this work to the Hospital in commemoration of its royal patronage.

The portrait of *Luther Holden*, c.1880, was painted by Sir John Everett Millais (1829-1896). Holden (1815-1905) was a surgeon at St Bartholomew's Hospital and was elected Honorary Surgeon of the Foundling Hospital in 1864, becoming a Governor in 1868. In 1879 he was elected President of the Royal College of Surgeons and even after retirement in 1880, he remained the Hospital's Honorary Surgeon until his death. Millais was an acclaimed Victorian artist and one of the founder members of the Pre-Raphaelite Brotherhood.

Opposite:
Fig. 35
Detail from Charles Brooking, *A Flagship before the Wind, under Easy Sail, with a Cutter, a Ketch and other Vessels*, 1754

Fig. 36
Joseph Highmore, *Thomas Emerson*, 1731

Rachel Moor: Baby 2,273

On 25 August 1756, a baby girl was born in the parish of Christchurch and baptised Catherine Laing. Her story is revealing, for it explains how and why very young foundling children were apprenticed to work.

On 4 September Catherine was admitted to the Foundling Hospital with two notes and a letter. The first note gives basic information about her date of birth and baptism. The second note appears to come from someone who had cared for her. In an educated hand it states that she fed well but 'without sucking', in other words she wasn't being breastfed, which was important information when it came to selecting her foster nurse. It explains that the circumstance of Catherine's parents was 'not sufficient to maintain the child', but that they hoped they might be 'in a capacity' to have her back in a few years. Finally it lists the clothes she was wearing on admittance. The letter has a hand-drawn device at the top - a unique identifier - and the wax imprint of a seal.

Catherine was given the admission number 2,273 and named Rachel Moor. She was sent to the Berkshire village of Wasing, under the supervision of volunteer inspector Mrs Draper. There she was dry-nursed by Catherine Loveday, who was older than most Hospital nurses and had four teenage children of her own. In 1760, when Rachel was four, Catherine Loveday and her husband Benjamin, who was a labourer, made an application to the Governors to have Rachel apprenticed to them. The Lovedays wanted to keep her, but Rachel had no legal right to settle in the parish. Catherine travelled to London and made her case in person. She outlined to the Committee the household's weekly income and the money her needlework for 'persons of fashion' generated: this was the skill she would teach Rachel. The Governors agreed to Rachel being apprenticed to the Lovedays, which meant she had right of settlement in the parish and could not be moved on by Overseers of the Poor. It also meant that while her long-term position was legal - akin to adoption - the Hospital could still maintain its connection. In the same year, another girl under Mrs Draper's care, Dorothy Prince, was similarly apprenticed at four years old to Mrs Mary Englefield, a mantua maker.

In August 1764, Alexander Farquhar - presumably the 'AF' of the device - applied to have Catherine Laing returned to him. Alexander was an insurance broker of St Michael's Alley, St Michael Cornhill, near the Bank of England. The legal bond of apprenticeship could not be broken without the consent of the Lovedays, who had cared for Rachel since birth. They must have agreed, because a year later Alexander wrote his will, declaring Rachel/Catherine to be, 'a daughter of mine…now at Mrs Ennion's boarding school near Blue Style in Greenwich', and maintained by him. The will states that at his death, his brother, George Farquhar Kinlock, a banker and merchant, would put in trust for her the sum of £500; the interest to maintain her until she was of age. In 1772 Alexander died, leaving his watch, sword and horses to his brother and all remaining money to his father. No other possessions or people are mentioned.

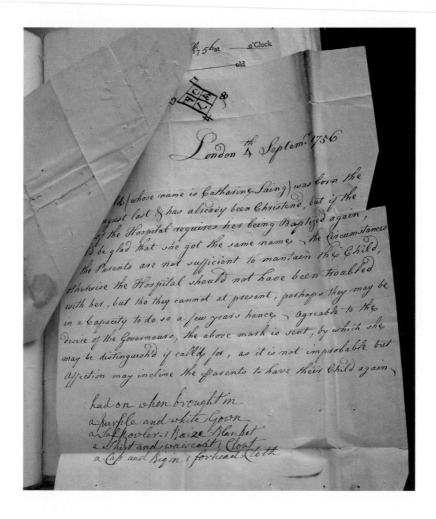

Fig. 37
Petition letter for Rachel Moor, Baby 2,273, admitted 4 September 1756

Fig. 38
Richard Wilson, *The Foundling Hospital*, 1746

COURT ROOM

The Foundling Hospital's Court Room is one of the best surviving rococo interiors in London. It was here that the Governors conducted their Committee business and entertained important guests. Hogarth is often credited with designing the overall scheme. The rococo plasterwork was a gift from the plasterer William Wilton, and its organic forms combine to great effect with the more geometric, Palladian elements present in the fireplace, picture frames and doorways. When Jacobsen's building was demolished in the 1920s, this interior was preserved and subsequently reassembled within 40 Brunswick Square.

A person standing in this room in the 1760s would have been immersed in the contemporary British art and design world. On display is the work of eight painters, a sculptor, an architect, a master plasterer and a mason. Much of the decoration explicitly references charity and philanthropy. The eight roundels depict London hospitals, the four large paintings depict benevolence towards children and the prominent inscriptions on the chimneypiece, marble relief and elaborate side table state they were gifted by their makers.

The marble relief over the fireplace was the second work of art to be donated to the Hospital, after Hogarth's portrait of Coram. *Charity* was made by John Michael Rysbrack (1694-1770), a Flemish sculptor who came to England from Antwerp in 1720 and remained in London until his death. Rysbrack and Roubiliac were the leading exponents of sculptural portraits and funerary monuments. Rysbrack's sitters included George II, Alexander Pope and Robert Walpole, the de facto first Prime Minister of Britain. He also created sixteen funerary monuments in Westminster Abbey, including that of Isaac Newton. This relief references the Hospital's social purpose and the ways in which the children could serve their country on land and at sea. Carved prominently in the bottom right corner is the Latin inscription 'Fecit et Donavit' (He made it, he gave it). Rysbrack's relief is set within a handsome chimneypiece by John Devall (1701-1774), who was chief mason to the royal palaces. Devall also inscribes his work with 'Fecit et Donavit' just below Rysbrack's and at the eye level of any gentleman resting his elbow on the mantelpiece. Opposite the fireplace is a carved pine pier table and gilded swag, c.1745, given by the architect John Sanderson (fl. 1730-1774). This is also prominently inscribed. The mirror was made by William Hallett in 1745 who rather ungenerously charged £3.15s.

The four large paintings in this room all speak to the theme of benevolence towards children and/or children rescued from peril. They are examples of history painting; the portrayal of a dramatic moment in a religious, mythological or historical story. Since

the Renaissance, history painting had been considered the highest form of art. In the eighteenth century, connoisseurs and critics were of the belief that British artists were incapable of mastering history painting. The decoration of this room presented Hogarth with a perfect opportunity to disabuse polite society of this idea. Although the result is not an unqualified success, it is fascinating to see how each painter rose to the challenge.

To the left of the fireplace is *The Finding of the Infant Moses in the Bullrushes* by Francis Hayman (1708-1776). Hayman was a prominent member of London's artistic community, a friend of Hogarth and a tutor at the St Martin's Lane Academy. Like Lambert [see p. 39], Hayman also worked as a scene painter, creating sets for Lincoln's Inn Theatre and the Theatre Royal, Drury Lane. Hayman was the artistic director of Vauxhall Gardens, President of the Society of Artists from 1766 to 1768 and a founder-member of the Royal Academy, serving as its first Librarian. In 1746 he donated this work to the Hospital and was elected a Governor.

In choosing the Old Testament story of Moses, Hayman and Hogarth could draw parallels with contemporary issues of child abandonment, rescue and adoption that the Hospital was addressing, since Moses was the original foundling. Following Pharaoh's decree that all male Jewish babies should be killed, Moses' mother placed him in a basket and put him afloat on the river Nile, in the hope that he would be saved. Having been caught in the bullrushes, the basket was found by Pharaoh's daughter who decided to adopt the baby. Hayman shows the moment where Pharaoh's daughter unwittingly hands Moses back to his birth mother to be wet-nursed. Hogarth's painting *Moses Brought Before Pharaoh's Daughter* takes up the story a few years later. Moses, now weaned, is brought back to Pharaoh's daughter who will raise him as her own. This parallels the Foundling Hospital's system of wet-nursing the babies in the countryside for the first five years of their life, before bringing them back to the Hospital. Hogarth's empathy for the distress felt by both the birth mothers and some of the wet nurses is apparent. For although he depicts Pharaoh's daughter as beautiful, kindly and able to provide Moses with everything his mother cannot, it is clear that Moses does not want to leave his 'wet nurse' and she does not want to give him up.

Fig. 39
Francis Hayman, *The Finding of the Infant Moses in the Bullrushes*, 1746

Joseph Highmore also chose a story from the Old Testament; *Hagar and Ishmael*, 1746. Hagar was a servant in the house of Abraham and Sarah. Sarah could not have children and consented to Abraham fathering a child with Hagar. When Sarah later

became pregnant, she ordered Hagar and her son Ishmael to be banished. Hagar, desperate and unable to watch her child dying of thirst, is walking away to die alone in the desert of Beersheba. Highmore shows the dramatic moment of salvation when God, having heard her prayers, sends an angel to guide them to water. A tale about a female servant being mistreated by a master who fathers her child would have spoken strongly to those who argued that foundling mothers were the agents of their fate. Highmore presented this painting to the Hospital in 1746 and was elected a Governor the same year. Highmore is best known as a portraitist – his portrait of Thomas Emerson is on display over the fireplace in the Picture Gallery [page 57].

Little is known about James Wills (d.1777), who painted *Little Children Brought to Christ*, 1746. He studied in Rome and helped run the St Martin's Lane Academy between 1743 and 1746. In 1754 he took Holy Orders and subsequently served as

Fig. 40
William Hogarth, *Moses Brought Before Pharaoh's Daughter*, 1746

63

Chaplain for the Society of Artists between 1768 and 1773. He donated this work in 1746 and was elected a Governor that year. This painting illustrates a passage in the New Testament, in which the disciples attempt to turn away a group of mothers who have brought their children to be blessed by Christ. Jesus then intervened saying 'suffer the little children, and forbid them not, to come unto me: for of such is the kingdom of heaven' (Matthew 19:14).

The eight roundels of hospitals in London were produced by artists Thomas Gainsborough (1727-1788), Edward Haytley (fl. 1740-1761), Samuel Wale (1721-1786) and Richard Wilson (1713-1782). In the eighteenth century the term 'hospital' was used to describe not only medical but also charitable institutions. These roundels place the Foundling Hospital within a long and eminent history of benevolence. Three of the roundels are by the artist and engraver Samuel Wale, who presented them to the Hospital in 1748. Wale studied drawing under Francis Hayman and was a founding member of the Royal Academy, becoming their first Professor of Perspective. *St Thomas' Hospital*, c.1748, was founded in the twelfth century as part of a monastery and named after St Thomas Becket. It is one of Britain's oldest hospitals and medical schools. Originally situated in Southwark, the hospital moved to Lambeth in the nineteenth century where it continues today. The original hospital's seventeenth-century operating theatre is open to the public as the Old Operating Theatre Museum and Herb Garret, in the roof of St Thomas' Church, Southwark.

Christ's Hospital, c. 1748, was founded by Royal Charter in 1553 to care for the orphans of poor Londoners. Built on the site of a former Catholic monastery which had been dissolved during the Reformation, Christ's Hospital was also known as 'The Blue Coat School'. Like the foundlings, children would be sent to the country for foster care, before returning to Christ's Hospital around the age of ten. In 1666 the Great Fire destroyed most of the buildings. Christopher Wren (1632-1723), a Governor of Christ's Hospital, and Nicholas Hawksmoor (1661-1736) were both involved in designing the new school. Wale paints Wren's building and in the background, the spire of Wren's Christ Church Greyfriars, where the children worshipped. In 1902 the school relocated to Horsham, West Sussex.

Fig. 41
Thomas Gainsborough,
The Charterhouse, 1748

Greenwich Hospital, c.1748, was founded by Royal Charter in 1694 as The Royal Hospital for Seamen at Greenwich and a counterpart to the Royal Chelsea Hospital for soldiers.

William III granted the Charter in accordance with the wishes of his late wife, Queen Mary, who had died that year. Christopher Wren and Nicholas Hawksmoor both worked on the project and the Hospital occupied this site for over 170 years. Between 1873 and 1998 the buildings were used as the Royal Naval College. The site is now part of the University of Greenwich and is the home of Trinity Laban Conservatoire of Music and Dance.

Richard Wilson donated two roundels; the *Foundling Hospital*, 1746, and *St George's Hospital*, 1746. The Foundling Hospital was still under construction when Wilson painted his roundel, while St George's had only recently opened in 1733. St George's was situated near Hyde Park Corner on the site of Lanesborough House, which had been built in 1719 as a private residence for the 2nd Viscount Lanesborough. St George's was a medical teaching hospital whose doctors included Edward Jenner (1749-1823), the inventor of smallpox vaccine, and John Hunter (1728–1793), the father of modern surgery. Like the Foundling, St George's stood in open countryside as this was considered a healthier environment than the city. They also shared governors in Dr Richard Mead and Lord Burlington. The site remained in use until the 1970s when St George's moved to Tooting, southwest London. Richard Wilson was born in Wales and is considered to be one of the first great British landscape painters, whose work influenced Constable and Turner. Wilson initially practised as a portrait painter, but after spending time in Italy in the 1750s, where he was able to study the landscapes of Claude and the environs of Rome, his career changed direction. He reached the height of his career in the 1760s, becoming a founder member of the Royal Academy in 1768. Wilson donated these paintings to the Foundling Hospital in 1746.

Little is known about the portrait and landscape painter Edward Haytley. His scenes of *Bethlem Hospital*, 1746, and *Chelsea Hospital*, 1746, are two of his best known works, due to the exposure they received hanging in the Court Room. The Royal Hospital Chelsea was founded by Charles II as a home for seriously injured or retired soldiers. It was designed by Wren to emulate the Hôtel National des Invalides, built a little over fifty years earlier by Charles II's rival, Louis XIV of France. The British Parliament had initially refused to support the project, requiring Charles II to find private donors to fund its construction. Haytley's painting gives a view of Chelsea Hospital and the genteel figures strolling in the grounds hint at the presence of Ranelagh House and Pleasure Gardens, which was nearby and on the Hospital's land. Chelsea Pensioners continue to live on the site. Bethlem Hospital, or 'Bedlam' as it was more commonly

Fig. 42
Edward Haytley,
Bethlem Hospital, 1746

called, was founded in 1247 and formed part of the Priory of St Mary of Bethlehem. It had treated people with mental illness since the fourteenth century, and until the eighteenth century it was the only public institution in Britain caring for mentally ill people. In 1676 the Bethlem Hospital moved to a grand baroque building in Moorfields which is the building in Haytley's painting. At its entrance were statues representing Raving and Melancholy Madness, which were classifications of mental illness at the time. Raving Madness struggles in chains, while Melancholy Madness lies unrestrained, staring desolately into the distance. Until 1770 members of the public could come and view Bethlem's patients as a form of entertainment. Hogarth was a Governor of Bethlem and he portrayed this voyeuristic practice in Plate 8 of *A Rake's Progress*, 1735.

Thomas Gainsborough was just 21 when he painted his roundel of *The Charterhouse*, 1748. He would go on to become one of the leading portrait artists of his day and a pioneer of British landscape painting, as well as a founder member of the Royal Academy. Gainsborough was born in Suffolk and came to London when he was thirteen to train with the engraver Hubert Gravelot. He subsequently studied at the St Martin's Lane Academy under Hogarth and Hayman, and assisted Hayman at Vauxhall Pleasure Gardens, decorating supper boxes. The Charterhouse was founded in 1611 by Thomas Sutton on the site of a former monastery. It served as a hospital for pensioners and a school for boys. To qualify as a resident, the pensioners had to be either a gentleman by descent and in poverty; a former military or naval serviceman; a merchant who had been impoverished by piracy or shipwreck; or a servant in the household of the Monarch. Gainsborough's painting shows the Terrace Walk and the Great Hall, with Charterhouse boys playing marbles.

Opposite:
Fig. 43
Interior of the Court Room

Fig. 44
Detail of John Michael
Rysbrack, *Charity*, 1745

Elizabeth Rainbow: Baby 4,104

Baby 4,104 was admitted on 12 April 1757, given the name Elizabeth Rainbow and sent to Ackworth Hospital.

On 18 May 1768 Elizabeth was apprenticed to John Bolton, gent, of Bulmer in the County of York, who was married with six children. Records of the time describe him as Irish and a former lieutenant in the West Riding Militia. His military service had been distinguished, but when the country returned to peace, he went into farming. In 1768 Bolton took on two apprentices from the Ackworth branch of the Foundling Hospital – Elizabeth Rainbow and a boy, Emanuel Bowes.

According to the *Criminal Recorder* of 1774, Elizabeth was 'remarkable for her beauty' and therefore 'enduced her master to seduce her'. When it was discovered she was pregnant, Bolton went to York to obtain medicine to induce an abortion. The medicine made Elizabeth violently sick, but failed. Worried that his family would discover his deed, Bolton waited until his wife was out and then sent Emanuel Bowes on an errand. When the boy returned Bolton said that Elizabeth had run away; later repeating the story to his wife. However, witnesses said that they had seen Elizabeth earlier that day and suspicions were aroused. Eventually the cellar was searched. Elizabeth's body was found buried, with her hands tied behind her back and a cord around her neck. She was eighteen years old.

Bolton pleaded his innocence but was found guilty of murdering Elizabeth on 29 March 1775 and sentenced to death. On the morning of his execution he was found hanging in his cell at York Castle; he had committed suicide.

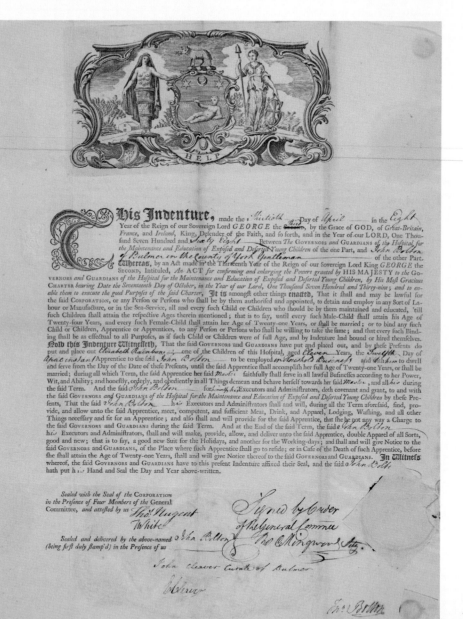

Fig. 45
Apprentice indenture for
Elizabeth Rainbow, Baby 4,104,
admitted 12 April 1757

HANDEL GALLERY

On the staircase to the second floor is a large painting of *A Piping Shepherd Boy*, *c.*1620–25, attributed to Tommaso Salini (1575–1625) and three portraits. These portraits were not donated by the artists to the Foundling Hospital, but form part of the Gerald Coke Handel Collection. Gerald Coke (1907-1990) was a businessman who assembled a substantial collection of Handel material. This is now a major research resource for the study of Handel and his contemporaries, numbering over 10,000 items, including manuscripts and printed scores, books, art works, programmes, libretti and ephemera from the seventeenth to the twentieth century. His collection was bequeathed to the State in lieu of tax by his widow in 1995, and formally allocated to the Foundling Museum in 2008. The Collection continues to add material and a reading room provides access for scholars and students.

The three men in the portraits were all closely connected to the Hospital via their relationship with Handel. *Charles Jennens* (1700–1773) was a wealthy landowner, scholar, patron of the arts and friend of Handel. A devout Christian, Jennens is best known as the librettist of a number of Handel's oratorios. His most famous libretto was *Messiah*. This portrait was painted in 1771 by Mason Chamberlin (1727-1787), who was a founder member of the Royal Academy. Chamberlin was also a pupil of Francis Hayman, whose painting of *The Finding of the Infant Moses* hangs in the Court Room.

The portrait of *John Christopher Smith* (1712-1795) is by Johann Zoffany (1733-1810). Smith was Handel's friend, secretary and copyist, in addition to being a composer in his own right. Between 1759 and 1768, Smith conducted the annual benefit concert of *Messiah* in the Foundling Hospital Chapel. He was the Hospital's first organist, and subsequently recommended the blind foundling Tom Grenville to the position. Zoffany was a German artist who had a very successful career in Britain. He was a founder member of the Royal Academy and he was well known for his portraits of famous society figures and celebrities from the theatre world. At the top of the stairs is the portrait of *John Beard* (*c.*1717-1791) by Thomas Hudson. Beard was a tenor, an actor and Handel's favourite English singer. Handel first spotted Beard's talent when he was a chorister in the Chapel Royal choir and went on to create several leading roles for him. Beard sang in every one of Handel's oratorios, including the first London performance of *Messiah*. When he sang at the Hospital's benefit concerts, Beard gave his services for no fee. Beard's second wife was the daughter of John Rich, the director and manager of the Covent Garden theatre. Beard helped to establish the theatre as an opera house and when Rich died, Beard took over its running. He and the Rich family sold the theatre in 1767 for the vast sum of £60,000.

Opposite:
Fig. 46
Detail from Thomas Hudson,
John Beard, *c.*1743

The plaster bust of Handel is a nineteenth-century model that used to stand over the door of the main showroom of music publishers Novello & Co. Novello's was the direct business descendant of John Walsh, who had been Handel's publisher and also a Hospital Governor. The portrait of Handel by the school of Thomas Hudson can be dated to around 1736, since the composer's hand is resting on a copy of *Alexander's Feast*, which was premiered at the Covent Garden theatre in February of that year. The portrait of the violinist and composer Felice de Giardini (1716-1796) is attributed to John Francis Rigaud (1742-1810). Giardini was a Governor of the Foundling Hospital and a prominent figure in London's music scene. He ran the Italian Opera in London, was a great friend of Johann Christian Bach and was responsible for a number of performances of Handel's work in the late eighteenth century.

Handel's will and the large case containing items relating to *Messiah* illustrate two important aspects of Handel's life; his philanthropy and his place in British culture. Like Hogarth, Handel was an artistic pioneer who experimented with creative forms. At the beginning of his career in London, Handel followed the prevailing taste for Italian opera. However, composing operas was a financially precarious business. A composer had to rent the theatre, hire the singers and musicians, and pay for costumes and scenery, so profits were not easily made. With his development of the English oratorio, Handel found a way to bypass the need for theatrical staging. Furthermore, having donated the organ, the Hospital's Chapel became a perfect platform for Handel's new musical form. With the success of his oratorios, Handel found financial stability and by 1750 he felt secure enough to make a will.

Handel's will is written in his own hand. He began to lose his sight in 1751 and the four codicils were only signed by Handel, having been written out by John Christopher Smith and John Maxwell. The third codicil of 4 August 1757 includes his bequest to the Foundling Hospital of 'a fair copy of the Score and all Parts of my oratorio called The Messiah.' A score and 28 hand-written parts were a valuable asset for the Hospital, enabling it to continue staging benefit concerts after Handel's death. The last codicil, dated 11 April 1759, was made just three days before Handel died. In it he leaves £1,000 to what is now the Royal Society of Musicians. Handel had taken part in annual benefit concerts for 'The Fund for Decay'd Musicians' since its inception in 1738. It would be another 100 years before the Fund found another benefactor as generous. In total,

Fig. 47
Mason Chamberlin,
Charles Jennens Esq, 1771

Handel's estate amounted to almost £20,000; a very considerable fortune. He left over 30 bequests to friends, family and staff, the first person to be remembered being his servant, Peter Le Blond.

In creating the English oratorio, Handel effectively established the British choral tradition. Whereas in Germany, a town of any size will have an opera house, in Britain there are choral societies. Unlike many artists and musicians, Handel's reputation during his lifetime was as great as it is today. He was the first composer to have both a book-length biography published and a statue erected in his lifetime – Roubiliac's 1738 full-length marble sculpture for Vauxhall Gardens, now in the Victoria and Albert Museum – and the first composer to have a complete edition of his work published. Roubiliac also designed Handel's monument in Westminster Abbey, a preparatory terracotta model for which can be seen in the *Messiah* case. In 1784 Westminster Abbey was the venue for the Handel Commemoration, staged to mark the twenty-fifth anniversary of his death. This 'mega-event' took the form of a series of concerts involving huge numbers of singers and musicians, establishing a taste for large-scale performances of Handel's choral work. In the case is a subscriber's ticket for the third performance in the 1784 commemorative festival, while in the table drawer opposite the case is a Commemoration ring from the same year, believed to have been presented to one of the first festival directors.

Many items in the *Messiah* case testify to Handel's popularity and his generosity. The manuscript score of *Messiah* was copied for the Hospital under the supervision of John Christopher Smith, in accordance with Handel's bequest. Nearby is a ticket for a performance of *Messiah* at the Foundling Hospital on 6 April 1773 which includes an engraving of Hogarth's coat of arms for the Hospital. The Hospital's benefit concerts of *Messiah* raised over £6,000; however, the publicity they generated would have been equally beneficial for the charity. The notice from the *Lloyd's Evening Post and British Chronicle* of 1758 is an example of the many advertisements for benefit concerts that over the years helped bring the Hospital to the public's attention.

The autograph letter from *Messiah*'s librettist, Charles Jennens, to Edward Holdsworth, a classical scholar, shows that the idea for the oratorio came from Jennens. Handel subsequently composed the score in just 24 days. *Messiah* was premiered in Dublin on 13 April 1742 at the New Music Hall on Fishamble Street. The performance had been at the request of the Duke of Devonshire, the Lord Lieutenant of Ireland, in aid of three local charitable institutions. The autograph letter from Handel to Charles Jennens,

Fig. 48
Johan Zoffany,
John Christopher Smith, c.1763

Fig. 49
George Frideric Handel,
Conducting Score for the
Foundling Hospital Anthem,
eighteenth century

Opposite:
Fig. 50
George Frideric Handel's Will,
Codicil three, 1757

dated September 1742, confirms, 'how well Your Messiah was received' in Ireland. The oratorio received its first London performance at the Covent Garden theatre in March the following year. The singers included a number of Handel 'regulars'; tenor, John Beard; contralto, Susanna Cibber, who was Thomas Arne's sister and England's highest paid actress; and soprano, Kitty Clive, who was one of David Garrick's leading ladies at the Drury Lane theatre. Unlike the acclaim *Messiah* received in Dublin, the reception in London was muted and Handel was criticised for having a religious work performed by actresses in a theatre. However, its subsequent performances in the Hospital Chapel secured its popularity.

I George Frideric Handel to make this farther Codicil to my Will
My Cousin Christian Gottlieb Handel being dead, I give to his Sister
Christiana Susanna Handelin at Goslar three hundred pounds,
and to his Sister living at Pless near Teschen in Silesia three hundred
pounds.

I give to John Rich Esquire my Great Organ that stands at the
Theatre Royal in Covent Garden;

I give to Charles Jennens Esquire two pictures the Old Man's head
and the Old Woman's head done by Denner;

I give to — — Granville Esquire of Holles Street the
Landskip, a View of the Rhine, done by Rembrand, & another
Landskip said to be done by the same hand, which he made
me a Present of some time ago

I give a fair copy of the Score and all the Parts of my
Oratorio called The Messiah to the Foundling Hospital

In Witness whereof I have hereunto Set my hand this fourth
Day of August One thousand seven hund.d & fifty seven

George Frideric Handel.

On this day & year above written
this Codicil was read over to the
said George Frideric Handel
and was by him signed and

Mary Lamas: Baby 10,125

In the early days of admission, before the use of receipts, distinguishing physical features were sometimes noted in a baby's billet, presumably as additional identifiers. These could be an impairment, unusual hair or eyes, marks on the body or skin colour. On 12 October 1758, a baby girl was admitted, given the registration number 10,125 and named Mary Lamas. Her admission billet lists the clothes she was wearing and has a scrap of blue and white fabric as an identifying token. It is only from a subsequent reference to Mary that we know she was black.

It is unclear how many black children were admitted to the Foundling Hospital, but there are references to others. For instance, one inspector wrote to the Hospital saying that although she was unable to take on any more children, she would be willing to consider a black child, such was her fondness for a negro boy who had died. In stark contrast, another child was physically abused by his nurse because of his colour and died from his injuries.

Mary was sent to nurse five days after admission, but she caught smallpox and was returned to the Hospital on 5 October 1763. On 27 January 1768 she was apprenticed to William Franklin(g) of Billiter Lane, Leaden Hall Street, London; a black cook in the West India trade.

Nothing further has been discovered about William Franklin. However, also living in Billiter Lane at this time was a major West India merchant, Sir Alexander Grant (1705-1772), who traded from Billiter Lane between the 1740s and the 1760s. Sir Alexander was originally a doctor who had been sent to Jamaica to treat slaves. He later became a slaver, amassing a vast fortune: at his death he owned 457 slaves and six estates in Jamaica.

Sir Alexander was a friend of Jonas Hanway, a Vice-President of the Foundling Hospital. Sir Alexander was also a Vice-President and supporter of the Magdalen Hospital – a charity set up to 'rescue' penitent prostitutes – arranging for some of its residents to start new lives in Florida.

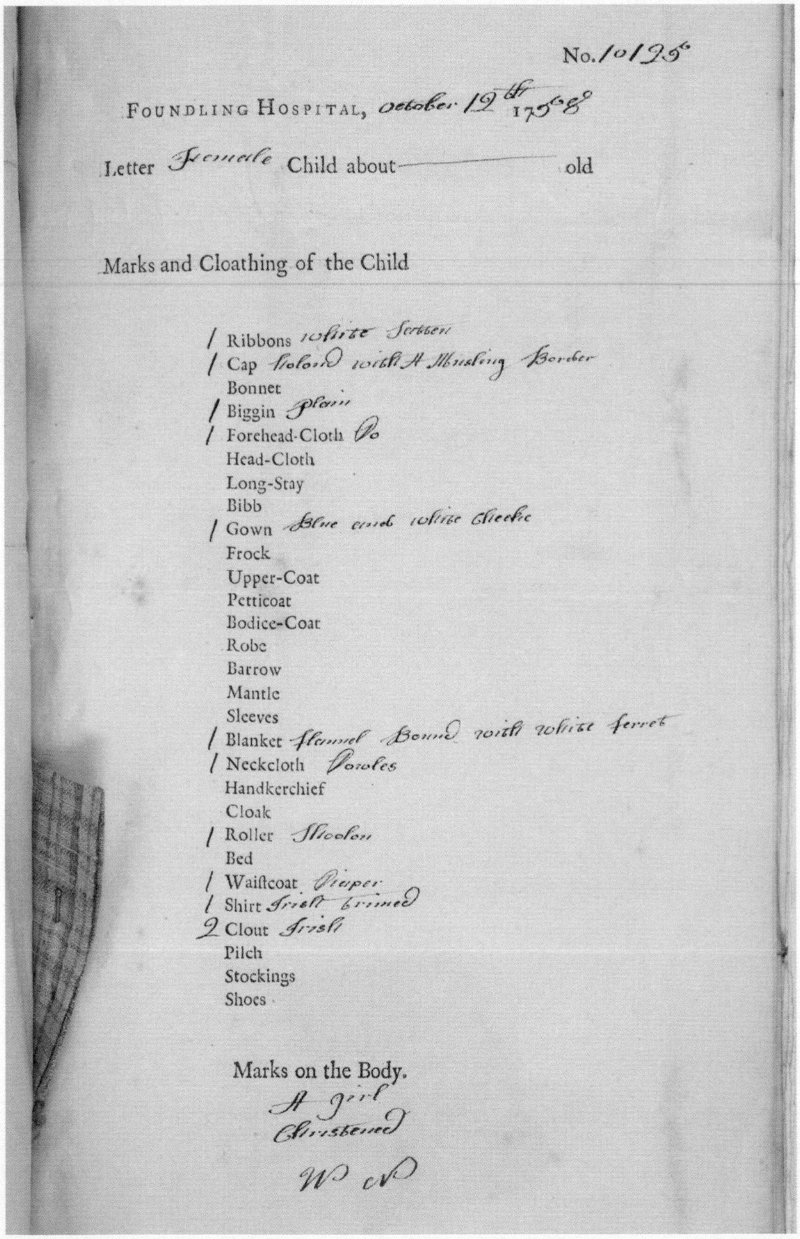

No. *10125*

FOUNDLING HOSPITAL, *October 19th 1758*

Letter *Female* Child about —————— old

Marks and Cloathing of the Child

1 Ribbons *white Serren*
1 Cap *Colord with A Musling Border*
  Bonnet
1 Biggin *Plain*
1 Forehead-Cloth *Do*
  Head-Cloth
  Long-Stay
  Bibb
1 Gown *Blue and white Checke*
  Frock
  Upper-Coat
  Petticoat
  Bodice-Coat
  Robe
  Barrow
  Mantle
  Sleeves
1 Blanket *flannel Bound with white ferret*
1 Neckcloth *Dowles*
  Handkerchief
  Cloak
1 Roller *Woolen*
  Bed
1 Waistcoat *Diaper*
1 Shirt *Irish brined*
2 Clout *Irish*
  Pilch
  Stockings
  Shoes

Marks on the Body.

A girl
Christened

W M

Fig. 51
Billet book page for Mary
Lamas, Baby 10,125, admitted 12
October 1758

77

THIS IS A TOKEN

I AM GIVING IT TO YOU

BECAUSE I HAVE NOTHING ELSE TO GIVE YOU

BECAUSE I AM VERY POOR

YOU CAN KEEP IT

AS A REMINDER THAT I EXIST

IF YOU WISH

OR YOU CAN EXCHANGE IT

FOR SOMETHING ELSE

AND FORGET ABOUT ME

IF YOU WISH

THE CHOICE IS YOURS

ARTISTS AND THE FOUNDLING

From early on, artists working in many disciplines were devising ways to support, promote and enhance the work of the Foundling Hospital. Remarkably, this commitment by creative people to get involved in the Foundling's work and help improve vulnerable children's lives is as strong today as it was in 1740, when Hogarth donated the first painting.

Hogarth and Handel were crucial in establishing the charity's public image and drove the ingenious creative philanthropy that took root. The Hospital's Committee minutes of December 1746 make it clear that the impetus to help came from the artists. Their offer 'to present Performances in their different Professions for Ornamenting the Hospital' would result in donations of painting, sculpture, concerts, plaster work, masonry, furniture, an organ, clocks and ironwork. These gifts transformed a utilitarian building into a major London landmark, a popular visitor attraction and an elegant venue that supported the charity's fundraising. By way of thanks, the artists were made Governors and met annually on 5 November 'to consider of what further Ornaments may be added to this Hospital without any expence to the Charity'. While some artists contributed just a single work, the support of others, like Hogarth and Handel, was ongoing and multi-faceted.

London's contemporary arts scene in the second half of the eighteenth century was rich and experimental. A visitor to the Foundling Hospital in the 1760s would have been able to see art by the best painters and sculptors working in London at the time. Then as now, London's concentration of wealthy patrons and dealers attracted artists from across the UK and abroad, including Allan Ramsay from Scotland, Thomas Gainsborough from Suffolk, John Michael Rysbrack from Belgium, Louis François Roubiliac from France, and Benjamin West from America. Similarly, the art world was small and artists studied, worked and socialised together, not just within their own disciplines, but across art forms. These creative links run through the Foundling Museum and connect unexpected people and objects.

One example would be the performer and theatre manager, John Rich. He is named in the third codicil of Handel's will [see page 75] above the bequest to the Foundling Hospital.

Rich ran the Lincoln's Inn Fields theatre in the early eighteenth century. In 1728 he staged *The Beggar's Opera* by John Gay (1685–1732), which was a runaway success. The money Rich made from *The Beggar's Opera* enabled him to build the Covent Garden theatre, which opened in 1732.

Opposite:
Fig. 52
David Shrigley, *Untitled (This is a Token)*, 2012
Donated to the Foundling
Museum by the artist

79

William Hogarth loved the theatre and his six versions of *A Scene from 'The Beggar's Opera'* are some of his earliest paintings. Made during the show's unprecedented run, these paintings immortalise the original cast and production. Subsequent productions of *The Beggar's Opera* featured Handel's favourite tenor, John Beard (whose portrait hangs on the staircase), in the role of Macheath, and musical arrangements by the composer, Thomas Arne. Meanwhile, in 1735, Hogarth published *A Rake's Progress* as a series of prints. Plate 7 shows Tom Rakewell imprisoned in the Fleet for debt, next to him a letter from John Rich, who has rejected the play Tom submitted.

Hogarth's friends, George Lambert and Francis Hayman (whose work hangs in the Committee Room and Court Room), were also successful scene-painters and worked for Rich. Lambert's painting-loft in the Covent Garden theatre was where The Sublime Society of Beef Steaks was formed, whose members included Rich, Hogarth, the actor-manager David Garrick, and the actor and playwright Theophilus Cibber, who was married to Arne's sister, Susanna.

Cibber adapted Hogarth's series of prints *A Harlot's Progress*, 1732, into a pantomime/ballad opera, which was performed at Garrick's Drury Lane theatre in 1733. The role of the Harlot was played by one of Garrick's leading ladies, the actress and singer Kitty Clive. Clive, Beard and Susanna Cibber sang together in the London premiere of Handel's *Messiah*, at Rich's Covent Garden theatre.

On his death, Handel left his great organ at Covent Garden to his friend, Rich; the bequest is recorded in the 4 August 1757 codicil of Handel's will. When Rich died in 1761, he left the management of the Covent Garden theatre to his daughter, Priscilla, and her husband, John Beard.

John Rich is just one strand of connective tissue that binds Foundling artists together. Others include Vauxhall Pleasure Gardens, which was managed by Hogarth's friend Jonathan Tyers and employed Handel, Arne, Rysbrack, Hayman and Gainsborough amongst others; and the Royal Academy of Arts, whose origin can be traced to the Hospital and its artist Governors.

Fig. 53
Detail from William Hogarth,
A Rake's Progress, Plate 7, 1735

This creative DNA continues to shape the Museum's work. In the same way that the Hospital's eighteenth-century supporters included painters, sculptors, musicians and clock-makers, so we work today with practitioners from many creative disciplines. They are central to the ways in which we reflect on the stories we tell and work with vulnerable children. The involvement of the 21-year-old Thomas Gainsborough in the Foundling story is another important precedent for us, and our artists range from recent graduates to established professionals.

The Museum's temporary exhibitions and commissions provide a space for twenty-first century artists and visitors to enter into a dialogue with their eighteenth and nineteenth-century forebears. Contemporary artists have been particularly adept at giving voice to the absent presence of the foundling mothers. Exhibitions such as *The Secret Staircase* (2008), featuring work by artist Caroline Isgar and writer Michèle Roberts; *Mat Collishaw, Tracey Emin and Paula Rego* (2010); and *Quentin Blake: As Large As Life* (2012), featuring work made for children's wards and maternity units, all explored ideas of maternal love, separation and/or loss. Artists have also been inspired by the resonance of 40 Brunswick Square as a physical space and as a repository for hidden stories of individual courage. John Kindness's exhibition, *An English Interior* (2008), responded to Hogarth and eighteenth-century painted interiors; while Terry Smith's multi-media installation, *The Foundling* (2009), examined the emotional power of institutional architecture. More recently, Clare Twomey's commission, *Exchange* (2013), provided an opportunity for visitors to not only reflect on the mothers' loss, the Hospital's promise of care, and the agency of the artist in mobilising public opinion, but also to take direct action. Finally, artists have found ways to fill the voids created by lost names and histories, with their own creative speculations. For our exhibition *Fate, Hope & Charity* (2013), DJ and poet Charlie Dark, writers Jackie Kay and Hallie Rubenhold, artist David Shrigley, and jewellery designer Alex Monroe all contributed work inspired by those eighteenth-century tokens that were 'orphaned' from their infant owners when they were removed from the admission records.

In 2008, the Foundling Fellowships were established, with support from the Clore Duffield Foundation. This biennial scheme is designed to celebrate the power of art to transform young lives. Every two years, three people are invited to be Fellows and undertake a project that speaks to the relationship between philanthropy, creativity and young people. The Fellows are named after Coram, Hogarth and Handel and to date they are Jacqueline Wilson, Cerrie Burnell, Michael Morpurgo and Lemn Sissay

Fig. 54
Tracey Emin, *Baby Things
[Mitten]*, 2008

HETTY FEATHER

One

My name is Hetty Feather. Don't laugh. It's not my real name. My mother chose my proper name. I'm absolutely certain she would have picked a beautiful romantic name for me (though sadly I have not turned out beautiful or romantic).

I shall picture her.

'My little darling,' she whispered, wrapping me up tightly in a shawl and holding me close close close to her chest, as if she could never bear to let me go. 'My little ... Rosamunde? ... Seraphina? ... Christobel?'

(Coram Fellows); Richard Wentworth, Grayson Perry, Yinka Shonibare MBE and Cornelia Parker (Hogarth Fellows); and Damon Albarn, Julian Lloyd Webber, Emma Kirkby and Chris Watson (Handel Fellows).

Each Fellow's project has connected with an aspect of the story we tell and shone a light on the talents of young people and the challenges they face. Some projects have been small-scale and the preserve of those who took part: Damon Albarn developed a workshop with musician Idrissa Soumaoro, involving a group of visually impaired young people; Grayson Perry worked alongside young Coram service users to create pottery reliquaries for display in the Museum; while Cerrie Burnell made a series of studies of single mothers through interviews and photographic portraits.

Other projects have involved casts of hundreds. Yinka Shonibare MBE's *Foundling Back to Front Weekend* transformed the Museum into an eighteenth-century fair, run entirely by young people. Richard Wentworth's *Soup for 100* was modelled on Hogarth's annual artist-Governors' dinner, and considered the impact that this conviviality had on the arts. *Soup* – which is now also an annual event – enables emerging and established creative people, who have a special interest in children's welfare, to meet and exchange ideas over a supper cooked by the Museum's staff. True to its eighteenth-century origins, *Soup* invariably ignites unexpected creative collaborations which, in turn, feed back into the Foundling's work.

Perhaps the most 'public' of all our Fellowship projects has been Jacqueline Wilson's book *Hetty Feather*. Wilson's story about the adventures of Hetty, a feisty nineteenth-century foundling, has grown to become four books and made an indelible impact on children's literature. In this way Wilson is following in the footsteps of Charles Dickens, another supporter of the Hospital, whose fictional character Tatty Coram brought foundlings alive for nineteenth-century readers.

The Fellows are standard-bearers for the work that all our artists do year on year to support, inspire and encourage young people to see themselves, the world and their place in it, differently.

Opposite:
Fig. 55
Jacqueline Wilson, *Hetty Feather notebook*, 2008

Fig. 56
Clare Twomey, *Exchange*, 2013

Luke Perkins: Baby 10,493

On 14 November 1758 a baby boy aged less than six months was admitted to the Hospital. He came with a coin, a piece of yellow ribbon and a note, written in an educated hand, stating that the baby had been baptised Oliver Luke. The writer took the trouble to describe the coin: 'a silver medal with a flower de lues [fleur de lys] engraved on it with this motto innocency in safety'. The coin is a Charles II shilling, minted between 1662 and 1685. Engraved over the profile of the King is the date 1758 and a pair of initials: RL and ED.

Oliver was registered as baby number 10,493 and given a new name, Luke Perkins. He was sent to Sarah Corral in South Mimms, Hertfordshire and spent five years as her foster child, under the supervision of a volunteer, Mrs West of Barnet.

In 1763, Luke's father came to the Hospital to claim his son. Revealing himself to be Richard Luke Esq. of Aynesbury [Eynesbury], Cambridgeshire, he brought with him a copy of the note and a description of the coin that had been left as a token. Luke was returned to his father; however, the Hospital required that he be given a similar training to those foundlings who remained in their care. This was to ensure that reclaimed children were given a good a start in life and were not removed simply to be used as cheap labour. In Luke's case he was apprenticed to his father to learn farming.

The Eynesbury parish records reveal fascinating information about Luke's father, Richard. He was born in 1704 to Samuel Luke, a gentleman. His wife Letitia died in 1752 and there is no mention of Luke in the Eynesbury baptism register of 1758. However, in 1754 Richard and a woman called Elizabeth Dixey were excommunicated by the Archdeacon of Huntingdon, for repeatedly and deliberately failing to respond when called to answer publicly about the 'crime' of an illegitimate child. This child, Peter, died in 1754. It seems plausible therefore, that when Luke was born, Richard and Elizabeth (probably the RL and ED of the coin) turned to the anonymity and relative safety of the Hospital for their son.

Sadly, three years after Luke returned home, his father died. Although no subsequent record of Luke or Elizabeth has been found, there had been a well-known Oliver Luke living in the area a century earlier. Sir Oliver Luke (1574-1648) was a Parliamentarian and a Member of Parliament, while his son, Sir Samuel Luke (1603-1670), was

Scoutmaster General to Robert Devereux, 3rd Earl of Essex and Chief Commander of the Parliamentarian army during the English Civil War. Sir Oliver owned a manor at Eynesbury whose device was a fleur de lys, which raises the intriguing possibility that the Charles II coin with the fleur de lys device, left as a token at the Foundling Hospital, was a family heirloom.

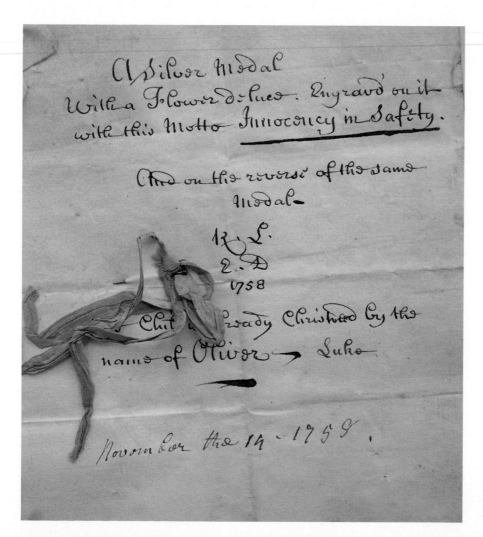

FOUNDLINGS ON THE EDGE OF TOWN

John Styles

The London Foundling Hospital was a ground-breaking, admired and influential institution. What marked it out from most of its continental predecessors was the fact that it was a secular foundation, funded by subscription, not by the state. Except for four years in the 1750s, the Hospital was entirely reliant on private sources of funding – subscriptions and donations. It rapidly became one of the most fashionable charities in London and was the model for a great slew of new, associational charities that transformed the way the capital's social problems were addressed.

These new charities were directed at specific issues, such as prostitution, juvenile crime, or venereal disease. They were funded by subscription, depended on public support and were organised as associations of the living, not according to the legacies of the dead. They also used all the new tools of an emerging popular press in order to raise awareness, including articles in magazines; newspaper advertisements for subscriptions and fund-raising events; and printed engravings of buildings and inmates. These new foundations fundamentally changed both how individual Londoners thought about their social obligations to the poor, and how the poor interacted with the institutions of the capital. They meant that the growth of a commercial, market economy did not result (as has often been thought) in a reduction in charity in eighteenth-century London. On the contrary, charity experienced growth, diversification and experimentation.

A high public profile was crucial for associational charities of this kind, as a way to raise subscriptions. The Foundling Hospital's impressive architectural presence was part of that profile. However, the Hospital was located not in the heart of London, but on its northern edge, in what was known as Lambs Conduit Fields. In part, the choice of this site was a matter of ensuring the health of the children. Its semi-rural location was considered healthier than the narrow, fetid streets of impoverished, inner-city rookeries that had escaped the Fire of London 80 years before. However, the Hospital's location also exploited the opportunity to command impressive vistas north from High Holborn, in the built-up heart of the metropolis, and up Red Lyon Street, the northern part of which was subsequently renamed Lamb's Conduit Street.

In adopting this location, the Foundling Hospital became part of an eighteenth-century version of what modern urban geographers term 'edge city'; a low-density concentration of business and recreational activities, in the liminal zone on the edge of a rapidly growing city. In 1745, the Hospital was one of the most impressive buildings in this 'edge city', but its location gave it some curious and unexpected neighbours.

A short stroll to the east of the Hospital was Bagnigge Wells. This spa and pleasure garden was a northern equivalent of the more famous Vauxhall Gardens on the southern edge of the city. Bagnigge Wells had an unsavoury reputation for vulgarity and loose morals – specifically for illicit liaisons between callow City apprentices and elaborately dressed ladies of easy virtue. None of this seems to have diminished its popularity.

A little further west was Tottenham Court. This was the location of the very popular and often very disorderly Tottenham Fair, the site of the Adam and Eve public house. The location and its pub were represented by Hogarth in his painting *The March of the Guards to Finchley*, which hangs in the Museum's Committee Room [see page 40]. At its rear, the Adam and Eve pub hosted one of the many tea gardens which thronged the edge of the city. On Sunday afternoons these were favourite haunts of Georgian Londoners.

In the fields closer to the Foundling Hospital was The Golden Boot, a small public house with a tea house and skittle ground. In addition there was the larger Bowling Green House, advertised in 1756 as commanding 'an extensive and pleasant prospect, and is fitted up in a genteel manner, with great alterations. Tea, coffee and hot loaves every day. The Bowling Green, which is in exceding fine order, is now opened'.

South of Tottenham Court, down Tottenham Court Road, was the site of George Whitfield's famous tabernacle, built in 1756. Whitfield was one of the most celebrated evangelical preachers of his day and a close associate of John Wesley, the founder of Methodism. He preached widely in both Britain and North America, but the Tottenham Court Road tabernacle was the hub of his ministry.

The Hospital's location in 'edge city' placed it right at the centre of one of the primary recreational destinations for mid-eighteenth-century Londoners. This was an entertainment zone, where Londoners of all ranks went for pleasure, whether moral, immoral, or simply innocuous, especially at weekends. It was a prime location for an institution which had to market its charitable mission to potential donors and subscribers, by opening its doors to visitors and hosting fundraising events.

For a while at least, the Foundling Hospital was the dominant presence among the confused architectural assortment dotted across this segment of 'edge city'. But eventually, towards the end of the eighteenth century, edge city moved on, as edge cities do. The Hospital was gradually engulfed by the remorseless northward march of London's serried rows of dwelling houses.

Overleaf:
Fig. 59
Thomas Bowles, *The north prospect of London taken from the Bowling Green at Islington*, c.1805. The Foundling Hospital is on the far right edge.